HOW TO UNDERSTAND
AND
ANALYZE YOUR OWN DREAMS

CONTENTS

Introduction

INTRODUCTION

We all dream and all of us are curious about what has brought on our dreams and what they signify. The fascination with dreams is apparent in prehistoric times. And in the Old Testament the possibility that dreams might foretell the future, if accurately understood, was suggested in the story of the ruling Egyptian Pharaoh during the time of Joseph and Moses. Divination, the art of telling the future or discovering hidden knowledge from dreams, palmistry, crystal ball gazing, and other magical routes of gaining information flourished. During the Middle Ages and the ascendancy of the Holy Roman Empire, dreaming was often considered to be the manifestation of supernatural powers, sometimes of good, sometimes of evil, or the invasion into the person of divine or bad spirits. Scientific studies of dreaming were virtually absent until nearly the turn of the twentieth century. Indeed, from the seventeenth through nineteenth centuries serious scientific attention to dreams was a low status pursuit. Dreams were of legitimate interest only to playwrights and poets, soothsayers, and any lay person who recalled a dream. Sigmund Freud's study of dreams around 1900 sought to learn the working of conscious and unconscious desires and conflicts, and his findings were a major step in the systematic scientific investigation of dreams.

Freud, through studying his own dreams and those of his patients, made the pioneering discovery that dreams, properly analyzed and understood, could be the "royal road to the unconscious." With Freud's discovery and the contributions of several generations of psychoanalysts since, a large body of information has been collected about dreams including how to analyze them and what they mean. This knowledge has largely remained in the minds of professionals—psychoanalysts, psychiatrists, and clinical psychologists—and has not been made available to the non-professional, in fact, to everyone who is interested in the meaning of dreams.

This book aims to provide this information to everyone. With this book, one will not have to receive psychoanalytic psychotherapy to get an idea on how to proceed with modern dream analysis. One will not require a disabling emotional disorder to pursue the intriguing adventure of exploring the complexities and depths of one's mind.

HOW TO UNDERSTAND
AND
ANALYZE YOUR OWN DREAMS

Chapter I

THE PSYCHOLOGY OF DREAMING

Before pursuing the interpretation of our first dream, a brief course in psychoanalytic theory as it relates to dream analysis is helpful.

A. CLASSICAL PSYCHOANALYTIC THEORY

Classical psychoanalytic theory, derived from clinical observation, holds that dreams represent a wish, often a disguised wish. Careful study of thousands of patients and their dreams supports this idea but, as one might expect, reveals that the wish is not usually readily apparent, especially if the wish or urge is not entirely acceptable to the dreamer. The wishful aspect of a dream has been classified as an expression of the *Id*, a psychoanalytic term that designates that portion of the mind which involves our biological urges and drives which are largely outside our awareness. The psychoanalysts' name for that function of the mind that works as a censor and inhibitor of our urges and drives is the *Super Ego*, and it, too, is largely unconscious in that its constraints were laid down early in our rearing in life situations which we have mostly forgotten. The *Ego Ideal* is another psychoanalytic psychological division of the mind, and it encompasses our aspirations, values, and those parts of our conscience of which we are mostly aware. The *Ego*, mostly a conscious mental at-

1

tribute, is the arbitrator between these different functions of the mind, the *Id*, the *Super Ego*, and the *Ego Ideal*. The *Ego* is a mental function that relates the total person to the real world and that takes leadership in striving towards the individual's goals.

These different portions of our mind and our mental processes do have some counterparts in our brain, in a very approximate way. But for our purposes here we do not need to bother about the details of this kind of information.

It is useful to know, however, that the process of dreaming, since it occurs when we are sleeping, involves proportionately more of certain unconscious aspects of everyday thinking and feeling (primary process thinking) than waking mental processes (secondary process thinking). Dream analysis is really a process in which we try to decipher the wishes and defenses of the dreamer by using our knowledge of primary and secondary process thinking.

Primary process thinking is a type of thinking which ignores the distinctions of time, place, or person; one time or place or person may substitute for another, if only vaguely similar in some way. Also, primary process thinking demands immediate gratification of biological needs, for example, food, sex, the expression of rage, and so forth, rather than postponing such satisfaction. External reality is ignored. It is a type of thinking more characteristic of the unconscious mental processes of the *Id* and *Super Ego* rather than the conscious, deliberative, evaluative, discriminative processes of the *Ego*. Primary process thinking is used much more in the mental processes of *dreaming* than *waking life*. It is more characteristic of the thinking of infancy and early childhood than adulthood. *Secondary process thinking* is much more precise than primary process thinking. It is characterized by the process of thorough differentiation between the times, places, and people that an individual has encountered. It is a highly discriminative and evaluative kind of thinking, always considering external reality and continually involved in decision-making whenever the individual is confronted with conflict-

2

ing motivations. Secondary process thinking is capable of delaying immediate gratification of various biological urges if reality factors or one's conscience so warrant. It is these features of the process of dreaming (the predominance of primary over secondary process thinking) that, at first consideration, seem to make the interpretation of dreams such an unsolvable puzzle. We will need here to learn some more technical vocabulary before we can begin to understand dream psychology.

In contrast to waking thought processes, dreaming contains much more of the work of the three mental mechanisms of *condensation, symbolization,* and *displacement.*

Condensation involves the process of abbreviation, the process of summarizing, of condensing, a process of mental shorthand which enables the mind to contemplate in a short flashback or playback of dream pictures or visual images, a brief version of a much more complex and lengthy series of memories and life events. In the waking state something quite comparable is that figure of speech (synechdoche) in which a part is used for a whole, for example, the word *sail* is used to refer to a *ship* as in "He had 30 sails under his command." By the psychological mechanism of condensation one can give expression to more than one impulse by means of a single dream symbol or image. *Symbolization* is a mental mechanism in which symbols are used to represent complex and elaborate events, such as, the use of a flag to represent a whole nation or a tiny cross to represent faith in an organized religion or the idea of being a martyr for one's beliefs. Both *condensation* and *symbolization* are mental processes that are manifest in waking thoughts and creative mental activities, such as, poetry and some prose. But, these processes are even more common in dreaming. *Displacement* is the third mental mechanism prominent in dreaming. *Displacement* refers to changing the object of an urge or drive from the original object, for example, hitting a punching bag instead of one's father or, more remotely, eating a piece of candy instead of embracing a forbidden lover.

3

Classical psychoanalysis looks at dreams from the viewpoint of the psychological conflicts in dreams, conflicts between wishes and desires originating in the *Id* portion of the mind and guarded against by the *Super Ego* and *Ego Ideal*. The mediator between these opposing forces and values is the *Ego* and the limitations imposed on the simple gratification of our urges by external reality, the real world. Either some external event (for example, meeting a new person) or, more or less often, some biological event (for example, a new phase in the menstrual cycle or too much or too little sleep) mobilizes or arouses some inner urge, usually forbidden, which immediately calls up from the memory storehouse of the mind all the parental and realistic warnings against acting upon such a wish. The outcome of this subjective conflict is usually a compromise of some kind and a disguising of the original urges by the use of such defensive mental mechanisms as *condensation, symbolization,* and *displacement.* Other mental mechanisms (pp. 6-9) also influence the contents of our dreams and our association to these contents.

To understand the meaning of a dream, the classical psychoanalyst would say that it is misleading to look only at the story of the dream as it is told by the dreamer on awakening, namely, the *manifest content* of the dream, for the dreamer's conflictual urges may be well hidden by *primary process thinking* and partial censorship via the dreamer's conscious and unconscious conscience.

Rather, the *latent content* of the dream, that content which was modified by condensation, symbolization, and displacement and by primary process thinking, must be sought. In other words, the latent content of the dream includes the motivations and conflicts underlying the manifest content of dream imagery reported by the dreamer.

Freud pointed out that even the manifest content of the dream may be distorted in the process of telling about the dream. The dreamer, in order to make the account of the dream more coherent or plausible, may inaccurately report the dream, leaving out significant items and adding new ones quite unconsciously to make the dream report more dramatic and logical. Freud called this process *secondary elaboration,* and he indicated that such elaborations must be recognized and stripped away before the analyst can probe into the unconscious determinants of the dream. This probing is accomplished by having the dreamer react to specific items in the manifest dream content with whatever ideas such items chance to arouse. The resulting train of *free-associations* will lead to some of the conscious and unconscious tension underlying the dream content. These details will be discussed more fully later.

B. NEO-FREUDIAN DREAM THEORY

Since Freud's contributions to our understanding of dreams, there have been additional discoveries that help throw more light on the process of dreaming. Most of these discoveries do not contradict what Freud discovered, but continue adding to our understanding where he left off.

We have learned that, even though the dreamer is asleep, a part of the mind is still actively functioning that deals with memories about external reality. This part of the mind is constantly surveying these memories to determine what courses of action in our past have worked towards achieving goals and those that have failed. So, in reaction to solving the present psychological conflicts between wishes or urges and inner inhibitions in response to such wishes, the mind tries out, whether the individual is asleep or awake, a variety of strategies based on past experience towards solving these conflicts. These strategies or coping mechanisms all consider, to some degree, the world outside of us, and they are associated in our memories with varying consequences. Memories of all the problems of living one has come up against and the coping methods used to handle them in our early childhood offer more simplified and less adequate approaches and are often associated with stronger emotions than memories of more re-

5

cent events. The earlier approaches to perceiving and dealing with such problems are usually, in fact, outdated and not quite applicable to the present day life situations. But sometimes—if some more modern, up-to-date psychological perspective and approach does not appear to fit the current circumstances—the mind tentatively tries out one of the more childish responses from our storehouse of memories. Using the psychological solution from our childhood to deal with present problems is called "regressive thinking" or "regression." Although psychological stances from our earlier years of existence sometimes are adequate to deal with present situations, quite often they are inappropriate and really do constitute a step backwards in the accurate appraisal of the present life situation and the best way to deal with it.

In any event, the scientific study of these facets of dreaming involves what is called *"ego psychology."* Ego psychology is partially, in fact mostly, a conscious process. Instead of a dream involving simply an unconscious wish (an Id impulse) and the opposition to it (a Super Ego demand) and its simple gratification, the modern psychoanalytic views about dreaming focus much attention on the various ways the dreamer's mind goes about trying out compromises between the conflicting differences of wishes and the demands of conscience and external reality.

In sleeping, as well as in waking life, a person is capable of using various mechanisms of resolving his conflicting viewpoints. In dreams, we can get evidence of how this arbitrating function of the mind works. There are so many different ways in which the mind makes compromises between various urges—say, sensuous and hostile ones—and one's conscience that it would take many, many pages to list them all. I will list and describe only a representative group of them here.

1. *Sublimation.* A technique whereby a drive is steered into socially approved channels of expression, channels affording outlets for tension, which help maintain the person's sense of being on an even keel. An example of *sublimation* would be to paint an oil picture instead of soiling with paint or in

6

a figurative way or to write a romantic poem rather than having forbidden sex.

2. *Regression.* A psychological process whereby a person uses ways of sizing up and adjusting to the world that were employed during previous phases of development. An example of *regression* would be for a 4-year-old child to start making increased demands for attention and to start wetting the bed after the birth of a baby sister. Another example would be the child-like enthusiasm and invigorating shift in values an adult experiences in going on a vacation or playing games or sports.

3. *Repression.* The psychological mechanism in which thoughts, feelings, or sensations are kept out of awareness.

4. *Denial.* A mechanism similar to repression, but it differs in that it is directed not against some unwanted impulses or drives from within a person, but against some disturbing aspect of the external environment or external reality.

5. *Reaction-formation.* The mechanism whereby an attitude or set of attitudes is replaced by opposite attitudes. For example, becoming a very active member of the Society of Prevention of Cruelty to Animals when one formerly used to enjoy teasing the family's cat and, before that, the baby brother.

6. *Projection.* The mechanism in which one's emotions, thoughts, or wishes are attributed to other persons or aspects of the environment. For example, a student who unjustifiably attributes angry attitudes of his teacher toward him because the student hates the teacher.

7. *Isolation, emotional detachment.* The mental process whereby the emotions and intellectual aspects of an experience are separated and the emotional aspects of the event becomes lost to awareness. The individual says, in effect, "I do not have feelings which might lead me to trouble. I maintain my distance, my detachment from emotional reactions that are dangerous to my welfare."

8. *Undoing.* The psychological process in which the individual tries to atone for or do penance or neutralize or erase

7

shame or guilt over some forbidden thought or emotion or the carrying out of some improper action.

9. *Turning against the self.* The process whereby a drive (usually a hostile one) is redirected from its original object and turned toward the self.

10. *Displacement.* The psychological process whereby certain drives or emotions are (unconsciously) transferred from one object, activity, or situation to another. For example, punching a pillow or dropping one's doll instead of hitting a parent.

11. *Conversion, failure of an organ to function.* The psychological mechanism whereby the awareness of an emotion or urge is suppressed and the function of a body organ, symbolically related to the urge, is lost. The unconscious psychological formula is "I will be safe from danger and self-criticism if that function of my body fails which I need to accomplish some forbidden goal." Examples are losing one's appetite when a person has a guilt-ridden urge to bite or "chew-out" someone or the paralysis of arm muscles of a violinist who dreads humiliating failure before an audience.

12. *Renouncing control.* The mechanism in which a person renounces responsibility for his thoughts and feelings and attributes them to an outside source.

13. *Avoidance of the situation (phobic defense).* This is a defensive measure in which one simply avoids situations that arouse anxiety. The psychological formula is "if I avoid the dangerous situation, I will escape pain and trouble." For example, a person dreads visiting someone because she expects to be dominated and humiliated. On the way to meet this person she develops anxiety and is unable to continue the trip. In this way, she avoids facing the situation which would put her face to face with the dreaded person. Physical illness may serve this same purpose of escape or avoidance.

14. *Wit, humor, clowning.* The psychological formula in this situation is "I am not anxious. The whole thing is a joke. I can laugh at it." For example, witty behavior may cover up

someone's distress. Or a young boy might clown to protect himself against feeling ridiculed and humiliated because of a deformity or because he is overweight.

15. *Dependence, desire for complete care.* The psychological mechanism whereby a person gives up one's independence and leans on someone else for support. For example, the individual finds someone who indulges him and looks after him.

16. *Safety in numbers.* A behavioral device whereby one puts oneself with many people rather than one or two, where there might be forbidden sexual or aggressive complications.

Ancient mankind, uneducated people of today, and educated mystics, lacking or disregarding the relevant data of modern science, have believed that God-like spirits or forces originating outside of us appear in our minds and dreams, control our thoughts and actions, battle within and outside of us for our body or soul, and even dwell within the inanimate world. Modern science takes the position that the actual truth of such ideas is not self-evident or proven and that such notions have most likely been acquired and learned through indoctrination by other human beings. There is evidence that the long period of childhood dependency of the human being and the very structure of our nervous system, itself (with its biochemical bases for memory, thought, and emotion) make us capable of wishing for magic, confusing us as to whether our inner mental life jibes with external reality, and of distorting reality to fit our own acquired perceptions, memories, and desires. This structure of our brain and our early life experiences impel us to seek closeness and affiliation with other humans and the hope of life beyond death. These views—once we have passed through childhood —originate primarily within the substance of the brain, itself, rather than from external supernatural forces. As these controversies between primitive or mystical thinking and modern science indicate, the human organism does have continual problems determining whether its ideas and feelings

9

originate within or outside of itself and whether its subjective experience (internal reality) accurately represents external reality.

The psychological mechanisms described above occur in everyday life, in normal and abnormal thinking processes. "Normal" and "abnormal" in this sense do not include differences in values, life styles, matters of taste or preference. The distinction between "normal" and "abnormal" thinking or behavior depends on the degree of distortion of external reality. Here, the term "external reality" applies only to perceptual and social events that are external to our own minds and bodies, events that can be directly tested and validated by other people. In this sense, the testing of external reality does not include the examination of evidence for the occurrence of events in the distant past, religious beliefs, beliefs in the occult, supernatural, or magical phenomena, for these phenomena are not capable of detection or measurement by scientific methods. Thus, a person could have strong religious beliefs and commitments and show no distortion in the appraisal of earthly or nonspiritual events and, hence, function within the range of "normality." On the other hand, an individual could be an agnostic or nonbeliever in God or divine influence, but could be functioning "abnormally" in that his testing of external reality was beyond the limits of his being able to care responsibly for himself and his other interests. Every person with mental processes falling within the range of normal thinking may occasionally show brief episodes of distorted thinking. Moreover, even when one's thinking is primarily "normal" there may be tendencies to use many of the above mental mechanisms. Conversely, in the most abnormal individual, there are areas of normal mental functioning that provide building stones for rehabilitation towards adjustment to real life, with its mixture of happiness and unhappiness.

The goals of psychiatric therapy, whether by psychotherapy, psychoactive drugs, rest, or any other means, involve helping people to adjust to life's stresses and strains and being as useful and productive a member of society as pos-

10

sible. All methods of therapeutic change work by decreasing the discrepancies between conflicted urges within oneself, inner, subjective reality, and external reality, or the disabling emotional reactions a person is having in reaction to such discrepancies.

The reader may raise the question what do dreams and dreaming have to do with the above matters? Since dreaming is a normal phenomenon, that is, it occurs with equal frequency in people who are normal, well adjusted and suffering no disabling personality disorders, how can dreams be a possible royal road to abnormal or psychopathological conflicts?

Freud did introduce dream analysis as a tool in the psychoanalytic psychotherapy of psychoneurotic patients, people whose everyday functioning was interfered with by disrupting anxieties, psychological and social inhibitions, or behavioral disorders. But he made his first advances in dream analysis by studying his own dreams over a period of many years and through this means he discovered his own underlying unconscious psychological conflicts. These hidden conflicts were well enough contained and circumscribed so that he led a highly productive vocational, domestic, and private life. Every human being has unconscious as well as conscious psychological conflicts; this is simply the nature of existence and life experience. People with disabling personality disorders have stronger and more such conflicts, and their capacity to recover from the strains of living and carry on productive work and human relationships are more limited than normal, adjusted individuals. So in the psychotherapy of people with personality disorders, dream analysis can give insight into areas of psychological conflicts they are not aware of, areas which may be contributing to their symptoms and signs of maladjustment. Likewise, dream analysis can give outwardly well-adjusted persons some ideas of their buried or unconscious urges or psychological conflicts.

11

C. THE NEW PHYSIOLOGY OF DREAMING

Through a completely non-psychoanalytic scientific discipline, two neurophysiological investigators (Aserinsky and Kleitman) noted that when someone is dreaming, their eyeballs move and may even follow the direction of the dream action. Since their pioneering discovery, considerable information has been acquired about the physiology of dreaming.

There are four stages of sleep, and these stages can easily be demarcated through brain waves, tiny electrical currents about 5-50 millionths of a volt, which can be recorded from a person's scalp with a very sensitive and powerful amplifier, called an electroencephalograph (EEG). During the second stage of sleep, which is a relatively light stage of sleep, these rapid eye movements usually occur. When they are present and an individual is deliberately awakened, the person will most of the time report that he was dreaming. Awakening the individual during the other stages of sleep will only rarely bring forth a report of dreaming, but often there are reports of less vivid mental activity than "dreams."

The first rapid eye-movements (REM) are associated with a distinct stage of sleep, REM sleep, usually beginning about 80 to 100 minutes after going to sleep. Clusters of these rapid eye-movements, associated with brain waves similar to those occurring during wakefulness, appear in cyclic fashion, about every 90 minutes through the night. On the average, people normally dream about 80 minutes over seven hours of sleep, and any one of these 4 or 5 dreaming periods may each last 10 to 35 minutes. Most of the dream experiences in normal sleep are never recalled. Some individuals claim they never dream. The fact is that they do, indeed, dream, but they cannot recall their dreams. Dream recollection is best when sleepers are awakened during the dreaming episode and becomes progressively poorer the longer they are permitted to sleep after a dream has ended.

Most of the rapid eye-movements occurring during dreaming are horizontal and these movements can represent a busy scanning of the scene of the dream action; yet at other times they may have no relationship to the manifest dream content. On the occasions when rapid eye-movements are vertical, sleepers sometimes report dreams that involve the upward or downward motion of objects or persons. When few or no rapid eye-movements are present, and the brain waves indicate that the sleeper is dreaming, on awakening the sleeper, the usual report is that some distant point in a dream was being watched. In other words, the amount and direction of the eye-movements can correspond to what the dreamer is looking at or following with his eyes, but not in a 1-to-1 fashion (mind-body relationships do not seem to work in a point to point correspondence of physical or physiological events to mental events, at least at the level of our current technology). Moreover, rapid eye-movements seem to be related to the degree to which the dreamer participates in the events of the dream. An "active" dream, in which there is much movement of any kind is more likely to be accompanied by rapid eye-movements than an "inactive" dream.

During actual dreaming there is an absence of large body movements. This seems hard to explain, but neurophysiologists have found that the large muscles of the body are "inhibited" or semiparalyzed during most dreams. This may be a mechanism for keeping the dreamer asleep in the face of the greatly increased central nervous system activity during sleep. Otherwise, the sleeper might thrash about or even act-out his dreams. One would assume that a sleeper would begin to move about as sleep lightens and that a good deal of activity would occur during dreaming. Actually, the opposite has been observed. Dreaming often begins just after a series of body movements stop. Then, the sleeper usually remains almost motionless, showing only the tell-tale rapid eye-movements, lip and finger twitches, and stirs again when the eye-movements stop. The sequence of events relating eye-movements, gross body movements, and dreams is similar to a spectator at a theater: fidgeting in one's seat before the cur-

13

tain goes up; then sitting quietly, often with rapt attention to the action, following the motions of the actors with one's eyes; then stirring again when the curtain falls.

Some body movement may be related to dream content. Sleepwalking may be an extreme expression of such motor activity. Sleepers occasionally vocalize when stirring, mumbling and even talking distinctly, but such activity usually occurs between episodes of dreaming.

External events in the sleeper's immediate surroundings may suggest some of the content of dreams, for example, drops of water falling on the skin or a ringing bell are occasionally incorporated into the dream content. Furthermore, stressful movies, compared to non-stressful movies, shown to individuals just before bedtime are more likely to stimulate dreams with anxiety or depressive content during the ensuing night. But these external stimuli all play on the storehouse of each individual dreamer's memories, eliciting more anxiety in the already potentially anxious person than the calmer, non-anxious person. I will elaborate later (pp. 18-19) in more detail about the relationship of the dream stimulus and the dream content.

Curiously, rapid eye-movements during sleep and, hence, dreaming have been found to be associated very often with swelling of the erectile tissue of sexual organs, specifically, the penis in the male and the clitoris in the female. These genital erections occur whether or not the dreams involve obvious sexual activity of any kind. There is a definite relationship, however, between certain dream content and the degree of penile erection. The more anxiety content in dreams the less the degree of penile erections. In fact, the more anxiety in dreams the greater the outpouring of adrenalin-like substances in the blood stream of the dreamer even during sleep.

Neo-Freudian dream theory and the new physiology of dreaming do not detract from the validity of most of Freud's more directly observable findings about dreams and the function of the mechanisms of condensation, symbolization, and

14

displacement in dream imagery as it reveals motivational conflicts. From these later sources we learn, additionally, that a dream image, e.g., a snake, does not necessarily have a stereotyped significance, but depends on the context in which it appears and the association it evokes, that dreaming is a normal and necessary physiological activity, and the dream scenes and drama can reveal how we cope with various emotional pressures and problems.

D. DRUGS AND DREAMS

Some people report that they rarely dream, that is, that they do not recall their dreams. We know that under normal circumstances healthy individuals have dreaming (rapid eye movement—REM) sleep on the average of four times a night. Why do they not recall more dreams?

The usual explanation is that they are personalities who shut out much of their mental life, including dreams. There probably are many people who disregard or who make a point of forgetting their dreams. Other individuals regard dreams as trivial or as noise rather than music and hence they do not try to remember their dreams. But another reason for not remembering dreaming is the effect of alcohol or some medicines on dreams. Moderate to heavy alcohol intake before bedtime can suppress rapid eye movement (REM) sleep so that the sleeper does not experience the stage of sleep that is associated with most dreaming. A similar effect occurs on taking the major tranquilizers, sedatives, or sleeping pills, a damping out of rapid eye movement (REM) sleep and, hence, a reduction in dreaming. The minor tranquilizers inhibit stage four sleep, slow wave sleep, and therefore do not interfere with REM sleep and most dreaming. But this slow wave stage of sleep occurs during the kind of sleep when some kinds of severe nightmares tend to occur. And so the minor tranquilizers have been used with some success in the treatment of recurring, severe nightmares. In time, we will probably make more discoveries about how drugs affect dreams.

15

Chapter II

DREAM ANALYSIS
AND INTERPRETATION

If really serious and valid dream interpretation were easy and a simple do-it-yourself matter, a psychoanalytically oriented book on self-analysis of dreams would have been attempted a long time ago. But dream analysis, even with years and years of special education and training, is not easy. So be prepared for some work on understanding your own dreams. I urge you to be patient and not expect easy or simple cook-book answers to the complexity or creativity of your own mental processes.

Let me try to give you all the information I can about the various frames of reference that the most enlightened and experienced psychoanalysts use when they start working on the dreams of a patient or when they pursue an understanding of their own dreams.

We will have to recognize at the outset of this adventure in the exploration of our psychic life through looking into the meaning of our own dreams that there will be limits to how far we can go. Freud, himself, discovered when he was trying to analyze and understand his own dreams that urges and motivations that he wanted to hide from himself because of shame, guilt, or fear resisted discovery, and as he got stronger inklings about some hidden psychodynamic process within himself from his dreams, his motivation to work on his dreams decreased, and he found himself avoiding such work. Or he became anxious or irritable as some new understanding about himself came to light.

A. DREAM STIMULUS

Although we are physiologically constituted so that we dream regularly about four different periods during the night, the specific content of these dreams is influenced by our current life events and the psychological conflicts mobilized by these events. Many psychoanalysts believe that the psychological plans, preoccupations, and conflicts of the individual are the primary factors influencing dream content. These conflicts make it inevitable that one or another aspect of the daily external events and scenes of our life will contain something that is relevant to our current psychological preoccupations. There is a lot of truth to this idea.

Many patients will tell their psychoanalyst that they had dreams precipitated by current events and that they think their dreams are simply reactions to these current events. A clever psychoanalyst may question such a statement by saying that since there are many, many external events during each day of the patient's life, how is it that only one or two external events were reacted to by eliciting a dream? Is it not more likely that each individual may be struggling, at any one time, with many different psychological issues and conflicts and that he selects from the events of each day certain ones to respond to with special significance?

Most psychoanalysts, in fact, prefer the latter explanation of the dream stimulus, but they do not disregard the fact that events in a person's life, if they can be pinpointed, arouse already latent or active psychological preoccupations. Hence, locating all the information one possibly can about the dream

18

stimulus will help us toward our goal in piecing out the deeper meaning of each one of our dreams.

Sigmund Freud called that portion of the preceding day's events which appears in the dreams the following night the "day's residues," by which he meant to signify that these events were singled out or filtered out of an active day because they had some special relevance for the potential dreamer.

B. THEORY OF OVER-DETERMINATION

A quite well-established theory of the hidden meanings in our dreams is the idea that each one of our dreams does not mean one single idea, but rather means many different things simultaneously. This should not come as a surprise, for the memory-bank portion of our minds has great capacity compared to all other species of living organisms. Our brain has a memory capacity far beyond any electronic computer yet developed. We now know from scientific studies that events in our lives—what we see, hear, taste, feel, and learn —are recorded in our brains as biochemical memory traces and that short-term memory and long-term memory are probably based on different kinds of chemical processes. In addition, our brain is capable of starting with the memories of every hour of our waking lives and coming up with some original and imaginative combinations of thoughts and visual pictures. These visual pictures that we end up seeing in our dreams are pictures and scenes that are so imaginative and different from what we anticipate that we sometimes forget our dreams are our own inventions, our own constructions, movies that come from our own mind, movies in which we select every one of the characters, make up the story, and direct all by ourselves, the whole show.

The plot of the dream, like a good poem, is highly symbolic and simultaneously represents many, many different aspects of our own lives put together from bits and pieces of memories stored in our brain. At one level, our dreams mean one thing, something very much on the surface of our present day comprehension and our awareness. And at other levels, our dreams relate to aspects of our childhood experience, long forgotten or even some aspects of the collective memory of the early dawning of the human race.

The latter idea is a viewpoint put forward by Carl Jung, a Swiss psychoanalyst, in a rather far-out viewpoint that mankind shares a "collective unconscious," that is, some ideas and memories originating from ancestors living centuries ago. Today, scientists cannot find strong supporting evidence for all of Jung's ideas with respect to the "collective unconscious." But scientists today do agree that genetics and heredity are examples of an unconscious kind of memory, laid down in the biochemical composition of our genes and chromosomes, in the form of complex protein molecules. These molecules, which are able to reproduce themselves, are able to direct and give messages to the physiological and chemical processes of our body, which dictate that our offspring grow to human shape and form, have a human brain, have the potential of behaving in some ways and not others, and are able to learn to speak (when other forms of life cannot communicate this way). Today, scientists think that memories of our past experiences have a chemical basis in some form of protein, similar to the chemical aspect of genetic memory and that even our very earliest experience are recorded chemically in our brain, though not always so easily recoverable.

So, our present biological understanding of dreams encompasses the facts that our dreams, in the first place, occur most often during a period when the brain wave patterns are similar to those of wakefulness, and interestingly are commonly associated with filling of the blood vessels in the erectile part of our sexual organs, and involve a complex symbolic sensory playback, mostly in visual form, of our past life experiences. Moreover, the *over-determination theory* says that there is not one—and only one—interpretation of

20

the meaning of our dream. Rather, there are many different levels of understanding of our dreams, some at different levels of consciousness and some at the same level of awareness but of a different psychological significance.

This observation that there are many different messages in any one dream should ease our concern and assure us that we need not fret about finding the only one and true meaning of the dream.

Each dream, then, is like an unexplored island, connected perhaps—under the sea—to other incompletely explored islands and to a nearby mainland. The dream is describable from many points of view as more of the uncharted and unexplored island and its surroundings are studied. Each further exploration and each new perspective about the island adds a bit of information about the make up of the land and what its composition is and how it is related to other geographical areas of interest.

C. THEORY OF CURRENT AND LIFETIME PSYCHOLOGICAL CONFLICTS IN DREAMS

Dream experts have discovered that dreams have some meanings that tell us about problems—external and internal —that we are having to face currently and in the here-and-now. These have been called "here-and-now" focal conflicts, which means circumscribed conflicts or small ones that may be very important to us now, but do not necessarily involve the main aspects of our life story or our life style. These current, immediate, here-and-now aspects of our dreams are very important to us in the immediate present and can—if understood correctly—tell us how we perceive (partly consciously and partly unconsciously) and how we are trying to figure out how to deal with some present life situations and emotional conflicts. These conflicts are, however, more like the chapters of a long book or one of the many scenes in a long play rather than the principal theme of the whole book or play when altogether.

The lifetime or nuclear conflict portrayed in our dreams, on the other hand, is one of the themes of one's life—the "story-of-my-life" part of a dream; this conflict is comparable to the main themes or messages of a novel or play. The lifetime conflict depicted in a dream is a psychological conflict that has extended through much of the existence of a dreamer, a conflict that evolved relatively early in an individual's life. It is a conflict which keeps coming back in many different forms to an individual as he has to face new life experiences or the memories of old ones and to cope with them.

The nuclear conflict of a dream usually involves the most central and deeply motivating drives in the person's life (for example, the wish or need to be loved and protected or the wish or urge to obtain recognition and achieve a sense of usefulness and productivity in human existence). The "conflict" side of this continuous conflict constitutes those childhood anxieties and other emotional viewpoints that appeared to present themselves as obstacles or hindrances to our realizing these motivational drives, however they originated.

Naturally, our here-and-now psychological conflicts in life (and as they appear in our current dreams) are influenced by our deeper, lifetime psychological conflicts, just as a book chapter has some tie-in with the underlying theme of a novel. In fact, current conflicts are often referred to as conflicts derived from other more basic or deep lifetime psychological conflicts.

As we learn to analyze and interpret our own dreams, we should plan to look for the current (focal) conflicts in our dreams and the older basic (nuclear) conflicts in our dreams. Also, we should prepare ourselves to find several current and old conflicts in our dream. It will be our intention to try to locate the most important current conflict and how the mind is trying to solve this conflict and, even, how this current conflict is related to certain older ones that have left their marks on our memory system.

D. COMMON FEATURES WITHIN DREAMS OF THE SAME PERSON. DREAMS IN PAIRS AND SERIES

A single dream studied carefully following the guidelines in subsequent chapters will give one an understanding of some aspects of the current life conflicts one is coping with and a glimpse of one of the earlier adjustment problems or conflicts in the life history of the dreamer ("nuclear" conflict). The more that is known about one's personality, life style, psychodynamics and life history, the more valid will be the interpretation that one arrives at of any one dream, namely, what life situations and inner problems it is trying to cope with and how it is approaching this life problem.

Repeated studies of one's dreams, naturally, can build up confidence in the accuracy and validity of the knowledge being obtained about one's conscious and unconscious personality make-up, especially when a number of different dreams from the same person provide information that support the conclusions one has tentatively drawn from the analysis of one dream. The point being made here is that dream analysis can be and should be done on a scientific basis. Data collection and analysis from the same individual over many periods of time and getting similar findings at different periods of observations are ways in which scientists establish scientific truths about individual human psychology.

Of course, there are special difficulties that one encounters with scientific studies on human beings because the human organism has such a large brain for its body size, a brain capable of storing more information than any other life form, and a brain which can put this information back together in new and creative combinations that are far beyond any electronic computer's capacity. This point is mentioned to alert the beginning analyzer of dreams that the manifest and latent content of a series of dreams may, indeed, deal with a similar facet of a person's deeper psychology. But dreams intervening in this series may deal with some other aspect of this many-faceted human being. That is, some dreams seem and are, on the surface, different from any of a run of dreams a person is having. These different faceted dreams have been evoked by the dreamer's reactions to an ongoing life experience that varies from the usual life experiences being encountered. Such an event might be an actual or possible birth, sickness, or death in the family, a promotion, a potential romance, an illness, a threat to one's self-esteem, an encouraging success, a frustration in human relations, and countless other everyday life experiences. And these life events evoke from each one of us quite personalized memories and styles of psychological adaptation, which in turn may generate a unique dream experience, somewhat different from the most recent daily preoccupations one has been having. These facts are spelled out to indicate to readers not to anticipate perfect consistency of dream themes in any contiguous time series of dreams, for irregular and unexpected dream contents may be retrieved from the less accessible memories of one's mind by various life experiences that cause specific chords in one's memories to resonate and become manifest.

I have tried to prepare the reader for a fair amount of irregularity, rather than regularity, in the meaning of dreams of one individual unless one covers a time span of several years of life experience where a relatively large range of typical life situations (but, of course not all) may have been experienced by a person. An individual in psychoanalytic psychotherapy, or some other type of psychotherapy, or a person who goes through a period of very successful or disappointing life episodes will, in addition, demonstrate prominent variations in the manifest and latent content of his dreams. This should not be unexpected for such an individual's personality is likely to be undergoing some changes of a substantial kind (referred to as "structural" changes by psychoanalysts) and, hence, there are likely to be concomitant changes in his dream experiences.

All these points are introductory to certain facts that

warrant attention regarding dreams that occur in pairs or triads in one night or in longer consecutive series over several nights or weeks.

As indicated earlier in this book everyone has on the average four periods of rapid eye movement sleep and, hence, dreaming sleep per night (except individuals taking drugs, including alcohol, antihistamines, caffeine, etc.). Usually people do not recall so many as four dreams per night, but more likely one, two, or at the most three. The psychological conflicts, conscious and unconscious, that these dreams are dealing with are almost always identical, but the defenses and coping mechanisms in these dreams may vary. That is, the dreamer tries out several different ways of handling the emotional problems that he is working on in his sleep. This is a helpful clue for understanding and interpreting any pair or larger number of dreams one may have had during one night; namely, look for the arousal of a common emotional concern or theme that the dreamer is trying to work with and solve.

Dreams in large series—for example, over days or weeks—may also be dealing with the dreamer's current working preoccupations. One may, as a guide, think of chapters in a book to explore how these longer dream sequences hold together. One sentence, paragraph, or chapter never tells the whole story, in all its embellishments, of a person's deeper and total personality. But the personal uniqueness of the dreamer may begin to be revealed with one dream, and this individuality will become more definite and distinctive as more dreams are available for scrutiny.

Dream content is influenced by biological rhythms (for example, the phases of the menstrual cycle), the use of psychoactive pharmacological agents (including drugs that are used commonly and do not require a prescription, e.g., alcohol, nicotine, possibly certain vitamins), and by endocrine, metabolic, or infectious illnesses. And certainly dream content may be affected by severe mental or emotional disorders. Nevertheless, a characteristically unique personal response trend occurs in the dream life of each individual, for instance, a suspicious, cynical person will tend to continue to be so regardless of the different biological factors influencing his mental and behavioral processes. An affectionate, hopeful person will continue to reveal these traits in his dreams regardless of external physiological circumstances. Exceptions to this general rule may occur in the dreams of individuals under the influence of some of the new psychoactive (mind) drugs, including tranquilizers, antidepressants and psychotomimetic drugs (such as, LSD), for these do appear to be capable of influencing the affective content or the degree of cognitive organization in dreams.

E. A CLOSER LOOK AT DREAM WORK: SYMBOLIZATION, CONDENSATION, AND DISPLACEMENT

There are some aspects of dreams that are common to all dreams, and this gives us a basis for generalizing about the meaning of dreams and for developing a general psychology of dreams and dreaming.

Let us reconsider, in more detail, the three primary characteristics of dream work or dream psychology, namely, the processes of *symbolization, condensation,* and *displacement.*

Symbolization

There are strong evidences of similarity in the process of symbolization as expressed in poetry and literature and as revealed in dreams. There are no reasons for us to expect, certainly, that certain brain functions that are active in the waking state, such as, creating poetry, drama, literature, art, and music are much different from the creative processes involved in dreaming. Indeed, the innovative and original manifestations of symbolic thinking in dreaming, that occur so unself-consciously and effortlessly while we dream, we would often like to be able to call upon and repeat when we are consciously trying to evoke the creative process in the waking state. Note, for example, these symbolic features of a group of dreams.

1. A dream scene starts out on the shores of a calm, peaceful sea, which builds up suddenly to a tidal wave that threatens to drown the dreamer's sisters and friends. The dreamer now becomes terrified and tries to rescue the threatened ones. Analysis of the dream reveals that under the dreamer's calm exterior is a surging powerful turmoil of emotions and urges which she is not sure she can master. The symbolism amounts to a simile that says, simply, under affectionate attitudes there are deeper emotions which threaten to harm loved ones.

2. A dream scene depicts briefly a college student carrying a briefcase with a weapon, a gun, hidden inside of it. Dream analysis reveals that the dreamer feels aggressively competitive with his fellow students. The dream symbolism includes a simile that says under the guise of intellectual and academic pursuit is hidden a rivalry with fellow students that is as dangerous as a gun can be.

3. A dream scene has a sixteen-year-old girl, the dreamer, partially blinded "because God has taken away his protection" from her. Dream analysis reveals that the girl's father and she shared a vacation together, in which the father and daughter had many long, pleasant conversations. He gave her some advice concerning her everyday worries that she found very helpful. When the vacation came to an end, the girl very much missed the close companionship and insights provided by her father. The dream symbolism makes the father all-knowing and all-powerful, like God, the Father, and equates becoming blind with no longer obtaining insights and understandng (to not see = to not know).

4. In this dream, a very small baby boy was climbing huge steps looking for his mother. He finally found her upstairs in a dark place standing very close to his father and not responsive to the child's cries. In reporting the dream, the dreamer felt an uncontrollable urge to cry and developed some transient, itching wheals, usually called "hives," on his skin.

27

Dream analysis revealed the dreamer was experiencing a deep sense of withdrawal of approval and unfair criticism by a Review Board, and his feeling of righteous indignation was incapable of actually correcting the error. The symbolism eloquently likens the dreamer's psychological situation to that of a baby boy scaling mountainous steps to reach a supporting mother; even when he finally locates her she is preoccupied with someone else and deaf to his entreaties. (The urge to cry and the skin hives have no symbolic significance, but are occasional psychophysiological accompaniments of feelings of desertion and hopeless rage.)

Condensation

Condensation is another facet of the mental transformations occurring in dreaming. It is similar and related to the process of *symbolization*, for these processes may both involve the use of a certain amount of mental shorthand to represent more complex and detailed memories, perceptions, cognitions, and emotions associated with life experiences. *Condensation* refers, specifically, to the representation of the whole of a psychological experience by a part. Our spoken language permits this process to some extent by supplying us demonstrative pronouns (e.g., "this, that, these, those") and indefinite pronouns (e.g., "it"), which words may refer to complex series of life events (e.g., as in the statement "it was intolerable," where "it" refers to ten years of living in Detroit, Michigan or two years of dating a boy friend). Our spoken language also makes readily possible our representing many phenomena or ideas by single words, such as, words referring to genera rather than species (e.g., fish rather than trout or mammal rather than elephant), collective nouns (e.g., crowds, millennia, century, infinity) and nouns or pronouns referring to constructs rather than concrete objects (e.g., wartime rather than soldier, beauty in contrast to you, and so forth). In addition, there is a figure of speech ("synecdoche") as I have already indicated, which permits one to represent a whole idea by a part, for instance, the use of the word "sail" to represent a whole ship. The process of *condensation* in dreaming partakes of many of these qualities of our everyday language use. An added feature of dreaming is that most dreams are composed of visual imagery rather than auditory. This means that various visual sequences, more than other sensory modalities, represent the thought and emotional content which the dream is portraying. Hence, shading and color may signify various characteristics. Moreover, brief, even trivial dream squences may summarize a major aspect of the dreamer's life style, some typical relationship with other people, or a habitual psychological conflict. These constitute the process of *condensation* in dreaming.

Let me give a few illustrations.

1. In a long series of dreams of one individual, some person in each dream was made fun of or ridiculed. This theme was a *condensation* of the dreamer's life-long attitude towards her father or any man who reminded her of him in everyday life.

2. A dream about dribbling and throwing a basketball through a hoop proved to represent a condensation of conflictual masturbation fantasies.

3. A dream scene of a woman receiving a blood transfusion which was inadequate to help her weakened state was found to stand for her unconscious wish that her husband would give her the love and support she felt deprived of since childhood and her feeling of despair that this "shot in the arm" or "refueling" would ever be sufficient.

4. A dream depicted a young man trying to locate and possibly rescue a young woman swimming under the water. Dream analysis indicated that this represented his search for his mother who died when he was a child and his tendency to look for impossible degrees of satisfaction whenever frustrated in his sexual life or even his vocation.

Displacement

The third dream process to be reviewed here is the psychological defense or coping mechanism of displacement, namely, the process by which one directs an unacceptable need or urge to a different object or objects than the original one(s). It is this psychological process which enables forbidden urges or wishes to be disguised in dreams by having them occur to unidentified persons or recognizable people other than to the self in dreams. The mechanism of displacement makes it possible for any dream character to represent some portions of the dreamer. Understanding the dream stimulus, the free-associations, and other details about the dreamer help the dream interpreter determine to what extent characters in dreams represent other people or psychological parts of the dreamer.

Some examples of displacement in dreams have already been given in previous dream samples given herein. But to remind us of just what *displacement* means, let us examine a few specific illustrations.

1. A young wife was deeply troubled by the impending temporary separation from her husband who was scheduled to be gone from home for two weeks on a business trip. Reared by her parents, particularly her father, to believe that self-sufficiency was a virtue and dependency a weakness and that being comforted and hugged when she was crying as a little child was unlikely to ever happen, she acted cool and indifferent under these circumstance, but felt vaguely uncomfortable and had difficulty sleeping soundly at night.

She dreamed that an acquaintance of her husband's had died and that she was trying to locate a good physician for him. Then the dead person phoned her and told her—in the dream—that the doctor she wanted to get for him was sick and dying and that he was not very competent as a physician anyway.

In this dream the dreamer displaced her unacceptable (to her) distress at being separated from her husband to her husband's dead acquaintance, thereby equating separating with dying. She also displaced her repressed anger at her husband (and originally her father) to the doctor, making him "sick and dying" and "not very competent." The dead person calling her on the phone represented a wish not to be alienated from her husband (or father) and, hence, a magical return of her husband (as if from the dead). The continued negative feelings towards persons not allowing her open expression of her feelings and who deprived her of her dependency needs is revealed in that portion of the dream content that indicated that the doctor was not a very competent one.

Usually, displacements of these kinds in dreams indicate negative and/or positive feelings that the dreamer is also having towards the self.

2. A young man reported a short dream that he parked his auto on a street, and on his return he found that someone had stolen one of his front tires. The auto turned out to be a displacement of (or substitution) for himself. The loss of a "front tire" symbolically represented his feeling that his ability was impaired in taking responsibility for and being decisive in taking a course of action that he preferred.

To know whether he deprived himself of the ability to steer his actions where he desired or whether someone else was the culprit would require considerably more information than we have available here.

3. A 5-year-old boy had a nightmare of being pursued by an angry lion. The angry lion was a displacement of the child's own angry feelings. He had been disciplined by his mother to control his temper and not say bad things to her. A child at this age is developing a conscience (ego-ideal and super-ego) and is usually working towards mastering his hostile impulses, and he fears their open expression may lead to the mother's disapproval and loss of love. Hence, in the dream this child disowns his own anger and, then, becomes fearful of his own angry impulses displaced to a wild beast.

Could the angry lion possibly also represent an angry mother or father at the same time? Yes, certainly, especially if there is evidence that either one of these parents has bared fangs, unsheathed claws, and has growled a number of times at the child.

4. A woman had a dream in which she took a walk along

31

a dark street and a man, whom she recognized, approached her and made sexual advances towards her. When she refused him, he tried to rape her, and she awakened in a state of fright.

The analysis of this dream revealed that the dreamer had unconscious wishes to have sexual relations with this man, but felt ashamed and guilty about these impulses. She *displaced* the sexual impulses to the man, putting herself in the passive rather than active position. As a potential rape victim, with the sexual aggression forced on her, this would help ease her conscience. If she were forced to have sexual relations and possibly got hurt, how could it be said that she enjoyed these intimate relations?

The dreamer was awakened by anxiety in this dream because she was partly aware of her own conflicting erotic impulses and because she did not want sex badly enough to be hurt in the process.

5. A displacement similar to one in example number 4 occurred repetitively in the dreams of a pretty, young woman who had anxiety dreams that an unknown man was hiding under her bed. Her husband, a successful traveling salesman, was away from home four to five days each week. Here again, the woman displaced her sexual longings—for her absent husband—to a hidden and unknown man. The externalization of her inner needs to someone else relieved her shame about her own sexual needs, but now she had to cope with her own hidden sexual passions displaced to an unfamiliar man, which violated her feelings of loyalty to her husband.

Chapter III

A METHOD OF SELF-ANALYSIS
OF DREAMS

From the preceding chapters, the reader now knows that dreams are psychological and physiological events in our lives that occur primarily during the second stage of four levels of sleep; that our dreams are accompanied by stimulation of our involuntary nervous system, especially if our dreams contain much emotional content; that very little muscular activity occurs during dreaming except the following of an action in dreams with our eyes; and that the content of dreams can reveal considerable information about our deeper worries and conflicts.

This next section will deal with how one can go about making headway on analyzing one's own dreams.

A. RECALLING AND WRITING DOWN DREAMS

As I have indicated previously, everyone has on the average of three or four dreams per night; and though some people claim they never dream, we do know that this is not so, but rather that there are simply some people who habitually do not recall their dreams. It is possible to improve one's dream recall by firmly resolving to study one's dreams and trying to recall them. For some people, a pad of writing paper and a pencil by the bedside will increase a person's incentive to write down dreams during the night, especially if one is awakened by the dream, or to write down the dream in the morning after one has awakened, before the events and activities of the day interfere with the memory process of dream recall. In writing down dreams, it is important to put down every detail, no matter how apparently trivial it may seem.

If a sleeper has had two or three or more dreams during the night, these should be written down in the order in which they were dreamt, again, in every detail possible. The setting or context of the dream, the background in the dream, the number of characters in the dream and what they look like and what they did or said or implied to the dreamer, whether the dream was in color or in black and white—all these details and many others should be noted.

Listing Subjective Feelings During Different Phases of the Dream. Now, there should be added to the detailed dream report of each dream, a self-analysis of the subjective feelings that the dreamer experienced during the night to each situation or activity in the dream. That is, the dreamer should ask himself, after he is awake, was he aware of the subjective feelings of any character in the dream that reminded the dreamer of himself. Also, the dreamer should write down any subjective feelings experienced during different phases of the dream by any other character in the dream than the person who most clearly represents the dreamer. These subjective feelings and their recall provide clues for the dream-analyst towards understanding the significance of the dream at greater depth. Also, their recall often helps the dreamer recover other portions of the dream content that have slipped away from awareness.

B. DETERMINING THE DREAM STIMULUS

In locating the dream stimulus, to start with, it is enough to ask ourselves what happened during the day preceding the dreaming or what has been happening over the past several days or week that seems important or crucial to us. In searching for these interesting details, it is more fruitful if one casually goes over in one's mind what seems to have been the important occurrences in one's life. If there seems to be several such events, the next step is to see whether these have some common denominator or whether they are all highly unrelated kinds of events. The next step is to note the exact feelings one had about these events, both the active urge or motivation and the counterreaction to it, for example, a wish to climb a mountain for excitement and adventure which may be in conflict with a fear of personal injury.

It is a good idea to jot down these ideas about current events which appear to have some connection with the possible dream stimulus. We will be using this information later on to pinpoint more accurately what psychological significance our dream does, indeed, have.

C. FREE ASSOCIATION ON THE DREAM (AS A WHOLE AND ON PARTS OF THE DREAM)

To do the next step in our dream analysis, we have to do some private free-associating. Sigmund Freud taught his patients to free-associate by instructing them with the "fundamental rule." These instructions for free-associating request the person try as best as possible to overlook the usual censorship we exercise over our marginal thoughts and feelings and wishes and to speak up freely about whatever comes to one's mind and to continue this process by uncritically letting come into one's mind everything of which the preceding thoughts reminded one. To get the best results in doing free-associating one has to suspend one's usual moral or ethical judgments or perspectives or preferences and allow to come to awareness any thoughts, feelings, or wishes whatsoever that might be directly or indirectly related to what one is momentarily concentrating on. While one is so doing, one should not keep out of awareness any bodily sensations or experiences. Rather these should be brought to awareness too and studied in more detail, for even these bodily sensations have some connection with feelings and thoughts we may have hidden from ourselves;

1. Free-Associating on the Whole Dream

First of all, one should consider the whole dream and allow to flood into one's mind every thought, feeling, desire, and memory that may happen to come. These may be jotted down for later reference.

2. Free-Associating on Dream Elements

After free-associating and noting all one can in this connection with the whole dream, then one should take even the most minute details of the dream and write down (actually or mentally) every experience or idea or urge that one is reminded of by considering each one of these tiny details. Many dreams have, in themselves, psychological issues or conflicts and, if these are obvious, the dream-analyst has a very helpful lead into the significance of the dream. He should, thus, free-associate as actively and productively as he can to bring up whatever memories, ideas, and feelings that he can about such.

3. Free-Associating on any Unusual Events or Details in Dreams

Quite often our dreams have funny or ridiculous details or rather unexplained features that, for the most of us, help us to distinguish the kind of thinking occurring with dreaming and sleeping with that occurring during wakefulness. These queer details in our dreams, these illogical or humorous or odd details in our dreams usually provide an important clue as to the deeper, more hidden meaning of our dreams.

36

D. SEARCH FOR COMMON THEMES

With the *dream stimulus*, the *dream manifest content*, and the data of your free-associations (*dream latent content*) loosely in your mind, now let your mind play lightly over these separate dream facets. Gently, without too much pressure on your thinking processes, *search for common themes*, common denominators, so to speak, associated with the dream stimulus, manifest dream content, and latent dream content. If you locate one apparently common theme quickly make a note of this. And, then, with similar light playing on your thought processes, look for a possible second theme that may run through the dream stimulus and manifest and latent dream contents. Note this. Next look for the third, fourth, or more common themes that seem to connect one dream facet and another. Note these.

You can allow yourself some confidence that these common themes, themes that overlap through all dream features, are substantial leads and clues to the current psychological conflicts with which your dream is dealing.

E. FORMULATION OF THE PSYCHOLOGICAL CONFLICTS REVEALED IN THE DREAM

Having noted these common themes running through the *dream stimulus*, the *dream manifest content*, and your *free-associations* to your dream, we are ready to try to outline the current psychological conflicts that have led to the dream script and subject matter.

Remember that psychological conflicts include some kind of wish, desire, urge, or need and an opposing motive (an emotion, attitude, or value orientation) that was aroused by the initial urge or drive.

We may now have enough information to arrive at some ideas of both the current and deeper, older lifetime psychological conflicts revealed in the dream.

37

F. EXAMPLES OF DREAM ANALYSIS AND INTERPRETATION

Let us look at some examples of dream analysis to get our bearings on how to proceed.

Example I

Dream Stimulus. "My friend J., at work got a salary raise the day preceding the dream and I did not. I congratulated my friend and covered up my envy."

Manifest Dream. "Some unrecognizable person had an accident on the highway and almost hit my car in the process. I was able to avoid being struck. I did not have time to wait to find out the identity or fate of the driver. So I kept on driving to work."

Free-Associations. "The dream sequence is strange, for it is not like me to shirk a responsibility to help a fellow driver out of possible injury. The other auto in the dream struck a stop-sign on the roadside and abruptly came to a halt. The front of the car was smashed in."

"I could not figure out the make of the other car. It was a bright red, though. My friend J., got a new car, two-toned red and yellow. He was boasting about getting a bigger paycheck than I. He has been a good friend of mine, but somehow I have not liked associating with him much anymore. I cannot recall any feeling I had in the dream except that I was a little irritated that this other car nearly ran into mine. The other feeling was an urgent one that I had to get to my job as soon as I could because something very important was going on there. Maybe it was something like guilt. I don't know. It is not clear at all what it was."

Common Themes. In waking life, the dreamer's friend, J., made progress on the job and the dreamer did not. In the dream, the dreamer made uninterrupted progress in his auto while an unknown driver came to abrupt halt and was probably hurt.

38

We will, from now on, assume that the various themes we can perceive running through the dream stimulus, the manifest dream, and the dreamer's association constitute conscious or unconscious motives, urges, or wishes of the dreamer, and these various motives will be listed.

Motive No. 1—Wish to get recognition and salary raise, but these were given to a friend and not to dreamer. (A wish frustrated by reality.)

Motive No. 2—Envy of a friend's success, an emotion not quite acceptable to the dreamer.

Motive No. 3—Urge to injure a friend (out of envy at his success), an impulse which is completely unacceptable.

Motive No. 4—Fear of retaliation from a friend (for having hostile urge toward him).

Motive No. 5—Unconscious guilt feelings originating from the dreamer's hostile feelings towards a friend (because having such a hostile urge does not fit dreamer's moral code).

In the dream, the dreamer covers up the identity of his friend (dream solution to conflicting motives) and makes him a stranger (due to guilt over hostile urge to friend). The dreamer pictures his friend's having an auto accident and having his forward motion stopped instead of these events occurring to the dreamer (an expression of the dreamer's hostile wish to "get ahead" of his friend), but in the process the dreamer (his car) almost got hit (fear of retaliation for hostile urge towards friend).

The dreamer unconsciously wishes to damage the front end of his friend (that is, his manliness, and this is sometimes referred to as a "castration wish"), but the dreamer fears retaliation from his own conscience for this hostile wish. The dreamer does not wish to get hurt, but there is fear of retaliation for his wishing harm to his friend. Also, his guilt over his envy of and anger at his friend makes the whole thought sequence unacceptable to the dreamer. So the dream proc-

39

ess changes an intolerable emotional struggle to an impersonal (isolation) accident scene (symbolization) on the highway involving some auto driver the dreamer does not know (displacement).

Dream Analysis and Interpretation

Current Psychological Conflict. The current conflict of the above dream example would be the wish to have a salary increase which is frustrated by the reality of the dreamer's friend getting a raise. This event arouses hostile envy of his friend which in turn mobilizes both the fear of retaliation and feeling of guilt.

Lifetime Psychological Conflict. The lifetime conflict would include the destructive aggressive urge (id impulses) to destroy a successful friend, and this urge conflicts with guilt and fear of retaliation (super ego reaction). It is likely that this conflict is the more general one and older one. The focal conflict (wish to get more salary conflicts with no salary increase for self but one for friend) is a variant of the nuclear conflict in this example, but need not always be so.

Example II

Dream Stimulus. "My psychiatrist, a man in whom I have confided a great deal, announced yesterday he was going on a two-week vacation and he will not be available to see me."

Manifest Dream. "I had a very simple dream. I was looking at a newspaper headline in very big print. It said 'Detective Shot and Killed!' That's all there was to the dream."

"I had no feeling at all about the headline except that here was another matter of violence in the big city."

Free-Associations. "There are a distressing number of shootings of police officers in this city. Actually, the newspaper headline was about a detective, a law officer who investigates criminal behavior. I think of Sherlock Holmes, the master detective who was able to solve many mysterious and puzzling cases that baffled others.

"My psychiatrist, in a way, is a detective, looking for clues to the secrets of my mind.

"But, why would I dream he was shot and killed? I don't dislike him. Could I feel angry with him? I know he's going on a vacation and will be away. It is unbelievable I would want him killed for this. The thought comes to my mind that the best defense is a strong offense. Would I want someone to get him first so that I wouldn't feel victimized by being cut off by him?

"In truth, I don't really mind missing some treatment sessions with him. What pops into my mind is that this situation with him is vaguely similar to an earlier one in my life when I was eight and my father accused me of taking my younger brother's marbles. It wasn't true, and I was hurt and angry with my father over this episode. I didn't dare talk back to him, though, for he didn't tolerate anything of this sort."

"I recall I was a little jealous of my younger brother's good looks and mother's obvious affection for him. But he and I got along well."

Dream Analysis

Common Themes. The departure or separation of two men from one another by fair or foul means.

Motive No. 1. The dreamer has a wish to be dependent on the psychiatrist about which he feels ashamed.

Motive No. 2. Furthermore, he feels murderous anger at his psychiatrist for planning to go away on vacation, and this anger arouses the dreamer's guilt feelings.

Motive No. 3. The dreamer's shame over his dependency on a parental figure and his guilt over his murderous rage lead to trying to forget (suppression and repression) of these unacceptable urges.

Current Psychological Conflict

The urge to destroy a frustrating father figure (the psychiatrist) cannot be completely put out of his awareness, and

41

the impulse returns in a disguised form as a murderous act to a complete stranger (displacement), an unknown detective (symbolization).

Lifetime Psychological Conflict

The dreamer had normal early childhood dependency urges toward his mother and father. He also had some envy of his younger brother and his possessions, which the dreamer was taught not to express. His wish to be the preferred child in the family was frustrated by his father's unwarranted accusations that he took possessions (marbles) from his younger brother. This life situation led to the arousal of murderous wishes towards his father for his inaccurate "detective" work about the stealing of marbles and the father's implicit repudiation of him. He suffered guilt over his murderous urges towards his father. The current and lifetime conflicts aroused by the dreamer's psychiatrist interrupting treatment to take a vacation are neatly encapsulated in an emotionally neutralized newspaper heading concerning a detective being shot and killed (condensation).

Example III

Dream Stimulus. The dreamer has just given up the idea of returning to college. He had previously dropped out because of being unable to finish some term papers. He obtained gainful employment for one year, something he had never accomplished before, always having been economically dependent on his father. Then he decided to complete his college work and get a degree. On trying to complete an unfinished term paper, he found he could not motivate himself to do so. In this setting, he decided not to return to academic life.

Manifest Dream. "I was playing in a baseball game with the Dodgers against the Padres. I got up to bat and hit the ball, but I was thrown out at first."

Free-Associations. "It's obvious that the Padres represent my father and the Establishment. The fact that I put myself on the Dodgers team is symbolic too—I've got some rebellious, though generally unexpressed, attitudes about my father's values. When I got up to bat, I couldn't even get to first base."

"I know my father was a great scholar and a self-made man. He has been successful not only in the business world, but also as a University professor. I do not want to follow his footsteps. Nevertheless, I feel I am letting him down by not getting a college degree. I am surprised that he seems to accept my not returning to college."

"It was my mother who encouraged me to be a writer and said I had talent. I think she made me think I was better than I actually am."

Dream Analysis

Common Themes and Current Psychological Conflicts. This dreamer gives us unusually useful and insightful free-associations. They practically give us directly the common themes and current psychological conflicts for which we are looking. So, the work of dream analysis in this example is relatively easy.

Motive No. 1. The dreamer has a conscious wish to complete college work and get a degree, but he is unable to complete his academic assignments.

Motive No. 2. The dreamer wants to compete with father and his achievements, but he is unable to successfully outdo his father. This inability to compete successfully with his father may be due to underlying shame (feelings of inferiority) or guilt (self-criticism and disapproval because of destructive aggressive urges) or both; there is insufficient evidence available here to know.

Motive No. 3. Conscious shame leads the dreamer to relieve himself of this unpleasant feeling; he seeks to do so by repudiating his father's values. A clue that he shares his father's goals and academic standards is revealed by his concern that he is letting his father down by not getting a college degree. The dreamer's surprise that his father accepts the

43

dreamer's not returning to college reinforces our idea the dreamer is trying to pass off his own shame to his father.

Motive No. 4. The dreamer's shame at a poor *performance* is blamed, now, on too much encouragement from his mother (projection), a further coping mechanism to ease his shame.

The metaphorical equation (symbolization) of a poor performance with a baseball bat and with a pen (writing) and blaming his mother for his ambitions with these instruments suggests an old wish for or possibly some actual seduction by his mother. With further study of this dreamer, if more evidence turns up of such a fantasied or real experience with his mother, this would provide a basis for guilt feelings about being too successful against the father (Padres), which is one facet of the so-called Oedipal Complex.

Lifetime or Older Psychological Conflict

Old feelings of inferiority about successfully competing with the father, and by extension other fathers, are present. There is a possibility that guilt feelings at wanting to eliminate the father also play a part in the dreamer's second-rate performance in the dream and as a college student.

Example IV

Dream Stimulus. "I just cannot imagine what brought on this dream. All I know is that it told the future."

Manifest Dream. "I had a wealthy, prominent acquaintance who was a movie producer. In my dream, which occurred many years ago, I saw a man in this movie producer's house. And he was doing something dishonest; it was not clear just what. I had never seen the man in the dream previously, but I could recall his facial features."

Free-Associations. "The man doing something dishonest in the producer's home actually did so one or two years later. At least, he showed that he wasn't to be trusted. I told my movie producer friend about my dream soon after I had it, and he just laughed it off. But a year or so later, when this man turned out to be untrustworthy, I reminded my friend of my dream. The peculiar thing is that the man in my dream was someone I had never seen before, and he turned out actually to be the identical individual who tried to do something illegal with my friend much later."

"I have no other associations to this dream. The whole sequence convinces me of the telepathic and prophetic nature of dreams."

Common Themes

There is a limited amount of useful and valid information from the dreamer's free-associations and elsewhere to draw on here. The dream was dreamt fifteen years before being reported to the author by a 74-year-old woman at a dinner party. She was trying to convince the author of the prophetic power of dreams. She may have lost or added relevant details.

If we take the dream seriously, the dreamer gives us no opportunity to reconstruct the life situations and context in which the dream may have actually occurred. Hence, we have nothing we can organize into a *dream stimulus*. Lastly, the dreamer, in relating the dream at the present time, seems more bent on proving her belief in her favorite theories of the telepathic and prophetic power of dreams, which also makes a good conversation piece, than on understanding the deeper psychology of her dream. We must consider some retrospective falsification has taken place. For example, maybe the man she claims she saw in her dream was not the same person she met for the first time one or two years later.

In summary, we must be cautious about doing dream interpretations on our old dreams or on old dreams that are related to us, especially when not much can be recalled about the life circumstances happening when the dream occurred or when very few associations are given to the dream content. With this dream, we should not try to make much effort on understanding it.

The only common theme we can elicit from this dream

report and associations is a vague warning to beware of trusting a man in one's home.

Motive No. 1. Strangers are not to be trusted in one's home.

Motive No. 2. Though the future may be uncertain, there is comfort for the dreamer in her belief that dreams have supernatural predictive capacities.

Current Psychological Conflict

The dreamer is preoccupied with whether to trust or not to trust a stranger (the author?) and let him into her emotional household.

Lifetime Psychological Conflict

Possibly her confidences have been previously trifled with or betrayed. She may be projecting her own dishonest urges into the situation. Her memory tells her to be on guard against strange men. Certainly, as one gets older, experiences increase in which one has been duped or has been tempted to deceive someone else. The origins of her belief in magical predictions to cope with the uncertainties of life experience cannot be surmised from the available information.

Example V

Dream Stimulus. The dreamer started intensive psychoanalytic psychotherapy with a male therapist after a nearly fatal suicide attempt by taking an overdose of a sedative. The suicide attempt followed the moving away to another city of a family upon whom she had become very dependent.

Manifest Dream. "I was with my mother by the side of a lovely mountain stream. A little girl about four or five years old climbed down the other side of the banks of the stream. She was in a pretty pink dress. My mother told her not to go down there. But the little girl paid no attention to

46

her and went to the side of the stream and slipped and fell in the water. The water around her became crimson with what looked like blood. I ran down the stream's edge and picked her up and she was covered with blood, and I thought she was dead. Mama said 'Let's rush her to the hospital; I think she'll be all right.' "

Free-Associations. "The little girl probably represents the child in me and my mother in the dream probably represents the portions of my mother that influenced me and have become a part of me."

"The child seemed to be unusually fragile. Her body was completely covered with blood. She had not suffered a bad fall. It looked as if she had merely slipped a little on some of the rocks and lost her footing in the shallow waters of the stream and gotten all wet. But the blood streamed out of her all over, apparently, and reddened the water around her. I picked her up, and she seemed to be alive, but quite seriously injured."

"That reminds me of an episode in my life when I was around four years of age. My mother and father were apparently working on making out their wills. I guess that they were trying to decide who might be my guardian in case something happened to both of them. So my mother asked me, 'Who would you want to live with in case father or I died?' I was dumbfounded by the question, for at that time in my life I had no interest in or intention of living with anyone else except my parents, and I had certainly not ever thought about their suddenly disappearing from existence."

Motive No. 1. There is a terrible threat to the dreamer's survival through suicide, accidental injury, straying away from a mother, or by death of one or both parents in her childhood.

Motive No. 2. The dreamer is like a fragile, easily injured child who needs to be and wants to be rescued.

Motive No. 3. There may be some fatal dangers, even though interesting, in exploring her stream of consciousness with a psychotherapist. (See Example VI.)

47

Current Psychological Conflict

The dreamer was attracted to exploring the interesting and beautiful stream (although the child does not go to visit the stream because of the presence of any humans there), but she fears that there are many *unpredictable* dangers in Nature for her and that she is unusually fragile and probably not capable of surviving the least threat of or separation from supporting people. The stream may also refer to her stream of consciousness and free associations (symbolization) that her therapist has instructed her to share with him. She is attracted to this process but fearful of exposing herself to serious injury.

Lifetime Psychological Conflict

The dreamer was severely traumatized as a little child by the callousness of her parents as exemplified by the unthinking questioning, when she was four, of her mother concerning whom she would want to take care of her in the event that both parents suddenly died. This and other related events shattered her basic trust in the reliability and steadiness of the love and support of her parents. As a result she was afraid of trusting and living for fear that she would be deserted or abandoned. She put up a defensive wall of disinterest in close attachments, and as a consequence of this defensive posture, she felt "half-dead" and terribly lonely. She blamed her own fragility for her sensitivity to separation or object loss (turning against the self) rather than the premature, fumbling attempt of her parents to prepare her for their eventual death. She defended herself against anxiety over separation by avoiding close ties with others and leaving them first so she did not feel like a helpless victim.

Example VI (Same person who dreamt Example V)

Dream Stimulus. Dreamer has a preceding psychotherapeutic session in which she becomes unable to free-associate,

48

reports she is also having difficulty in her academic work, and lapses into silence.

Manifest Dream. "My sister and I were at home when my brother and a companion of his came into the house. It was clear that they intended to kill us. I felt resigned and did not put up a struggle. My brother succeeded in blinding me, but not killing me. My sister escaped injury. My brother and his companion ran out of the house."

Free Associations. "I felt there was some justification for my brother's action and no good reason to defend myself. You see, my brother was the youngest of us three children. I was the oldest and my sister was second. I liked academic achievement and did well at school and my sister was a social success. That made it very difficult for my brother to emulate us successfully, and he disappointed my parents' ambitions for him, both in the academic and social areas. I can understand why he would want to kill both of us."

"Blindness I associate with not being able to see, blocking out understanding, interfering with intellectual processes."

Motive No. 1. For excessive wisdom and insight, one should feel guilty and be punished.

Motive No. 2. One way to atone for being a smarter student than a brother is to lose one's vision and, hence, understanding.

Motive No. 3. A brother might want to kill or blind the dreamer for being so competitive (projection).

Lifetime Psychological Conflict

Feelings of intellectual competition with her male therapist (and other brother figures in her life) caused her to fear retaliation and threat to her life or her ability to see and understand. To protect herself against these emotional conflicts over competition with men she renounced her abilities to free-associate and to perform well academically.

49

Current Psychological Conflict

The current psychological conflict is mirrored in her childhood experiences with her brother. She consciously felt protective of her brother and guilty over the unfavorable comparisons made by her parents with respect to his academic achievement in contrast to hers. She has completely forgotten, as an older sister, her own very early competitive feelings toward him for the love of her parents when he and she were much younger.

The relating of many dreams and the analysis of the personal meaning and significance of these dreams does not provide a sure blue-print to the solution of the problem of dream analysis. Why? Because dreams are so strongly stamped with the characteristics of the individual dreamer. This fact requires our knowing as much as we can about the individual dreamer and the life situation in which he is involved, which forms the context of each dream. In other words, the more one knows about the life experiences of a dreamer, the more understandable become the details and meanings of one's dreams.

There is no way to dispense with these aspects of understanding dreams, and I will stress this feature of dreams in the next chapter, while simultaneously illustrating some of the aspects of dreams which typify all dreams.

Chapter IV

FOLLOWING A SERIES OF DREAMS

As has been pointed out previously here, a single dream carefully studied will give an understanding of some of the current, psychological conflicts with which one is coping, but only a hint of the older lifetime conflicts that one has had to face. The analysis of many dreams from the same individual, on the other hand, can give a fuller view of these lifetime conflicts, while illustrating the variety of psychological maneuvers the dreamer uses to adjust to day-to-day stressful situations.

Example I

To get a more thorough view of oneself, including the complexities of one's personality makeup and the extent to which a person can change in adjustment patterns with the passage of time or in response to a therapeutic agent, the analysis of a series of dreams from one individual is useful. As a beginning, let us study a short series of dreams from one young man, a college student. Unfortunately, we have no free-associations on these dreams; so that we have no way to look into the extent to which and in what ways these dreams have undergone some distortion and covering up (secondary elaboration) of the original manifest dream content. Without free-associations we will be hindered, somewhat, in getting at the latent dream content. The dreams were all dreamt within a one-week period and written down by the dreamer. He was a student in his early twenties who lived at home with his parents, who had very little social life, and who was very shy with women. He aspired to be a writer or movie director.

Dream Series I

Dream Stimulus. The dreamer had just sought his father's opinion about his desire to quit college and get a job, though he had never before had any gainful employment.

Dream No. 1. "A girl was telling me to be more frank with my father and to tell him of my reservations about the helpfulness of his advice regarding my dropping out of school."

Dream No. 2. "I was in the mountains, this was around the age of my high school days, and I was being hunted down by Indians. They had bows and arrows, and one almost got me. I was afraid the Indians would cut my throat. The scene changed and I was at my high school, and I was running in between houses, trying to get away from the Indians. My friend, Charlie, was with me, and I asked how he planned to get away. He said he was trying to go it on his own and escape solo. I said, 'I have tried that but you know, you get hungry after a while.' Charlie laughed."

"Next scene was at an eating area where we could get a free dinner. Charlie was sitting about four seats away on a bench. The guy ahead of him wiped some food on Charlie's face and said, 'Pass it on.' This piece of food eventually found its way to the chap next to me, and after taking a sample of it, he put it on my face and spoke the words, 'Pass it on.' I decided not to pass it on, but placed it back on the guy who had put it on me, and said, 'What's this about?' "

Dream No. 3. "Again, this dream went back to the time I was with Charlie. We went into a store with the plan of getting some grass. The woman there laid it on the counter, I gave her $20, she took it and confusedly returned about

$40 to me. Then an oldish couple walked into the store, and they looked like narcs. So Charlie and I just left the stuff on the counter and walked out."

Dream No. 4. "Inside some auditorium, there was a girl with her boy friend and he was in his late twenties and had a full beard. We were going to play some records, and I had some of my albums there, and I went through them to see which to play that might impress them. Then another girl was there laughing and making a pass at me. I had somewhere picked up somebody's key chain, and on it was a nude female figure. The girl looked at it and laughed.

"Then later on I had to leave the auditorium. When I came back, I was afraid some of my record albums were stolen. I checked, and some were."

Dream No. 5. "This dream started on a street, it was at night, and police were walking down the street with guns and started arresting many people. I ran and turned the corner and the panicked, crowded, throbbing night scene changed."

"There was an old store, and a young girl with big eyes looked at me and asked if she could stay with me. Then her mother came up to me, and I said, 'You have an aggressive daughter.' I acted kind of cool and wanted to show the mom that I was no tough guy. But at the same time, I wanted to take the little girl home. The mother left, and then I looked at the girl and motioned for her to follow me. She started to follow me and then hesitated. At this point, I woke up."

"At the beginning of this dream, some of these people and I seemed to be up on a mock stage. I can't recall what we were doing up there, but I remember that there were a lot of people around watching us, and we were having a great time."

Since we do not have access to the dreamer's free associations to these dreams, although we do have an event just preceding the dreams that probably served as a stimulus for the dreams, we will look for common themes only in the dream stimulus and all the ensuing dreams. This will give us

53

some general ideas what inner needs and conflicts this dreaming activity was trying to solve.

Common Themes

With the dream stimulus, the young man is faced with the problem of justifying to his father his desire to discontinue his education and get a job. In so doing, he recognizes the fact that he has had no previous experience in gainful employment.

Dream No. 1. The dreamer has someone advising him, a girl, that he should be more opened about his dislike of his father's efforts to help him come to a decision about dropping out of school; there is a suggestion that he is covering up his true feelings about his father's advice. Unfortunately, we do not know, from the information we have to work with, what the father's advice really was.

Dream No. 2. There is a fear of being killed by arrows or throat-cutting (oral reference) by wild Indians (an expression of his severe conscience, his super ego, which is displaced to others). Just what is the urge, the motivation, which is evoking such a strong reaction from his conscience in the form of a fear of retaliation is not, at this point, clear. Apparently, the unacceptable motivation is embedded in his wish to drop out of college. Possibly, the fear of getting his throat cut provides a clue, in that he sensed (unconsciously) some urge associated with the throat and feeding, getting fed, or being nurtured (symbolization) and dropping out of school.

In his isolation and loneliness, he changes the scene to one in which he has a companion, Charlie (misery loves company), with whom he is sharing the punishment of conscience.

Some joking and humor is provided in this dream, which eases the emotional strain he is apparently experiencing, and this humor is supposed to help him deal with what we discover is "hunger" (burdened with possible shame), and it appears that there is something about this hunger which makes him worry about suffering the attacks of his unbridled conscience (wild Indians) in the company of a male companion rather than alone.

The theme of becoming hungry and getting free food is now clearly introduced (possibly representing the dreamer's continuing wish to be on the receiving end and be supplied with support from his father or any other available sources).

A slapstick quality now develops in the dreaming process with the idea of men eating together by smearing food on each other's face (more use of wit and humor to deal with difficult inner problems). In addition, the dreamer comes up with the argument that he is not alone or unique in wanting to be fed, for many other men, as well as he, line up for free food (which serves to decrease his own shame about wanting to be taken care of).

A hint that this feeding chain (and everything it may symbolize) is not entirely comfortable to him is again provided by his not going along with all of it.

Dream No. 3. The theme of getting something for nothing recurs—he is about to get some marihuana and money free. In dream No. 1 a girl and a father gave him something—advice. In dream No. 2, free food was made available.

The theme of companionship recurs—he is not alone, but with Charlie.

The theme of getting caught in an illegal action (getting an illegal substance which is taken by mouth for pleasure) is introduced, but maybe the idea that his wish to quit school has an illegal component (at least for his conscience) is already hinted at in dream No. 2 when he dreamt about Indians wanting to cut his throat.

The theme of covering up recurs, and now it is these hidden oral aims that he and his friend want to disown from some older (parental) couple, the narcs.

Dream No. 4. Now there appears a wish to impress a young couple by playing his records (mild exhibitionistic urge for attention).

The theme of getting something free reappears—this time in the form of a girl who offers him free sex.

55

Borrowing or taking somebody's key ring with a nude woman on it is a puzzling detail, suggesting perhaps he needs some other male along with him to back him up on a heterosexual enterprise.

The theme of someone stealing his records is similar to previous references to possible hostility of others towards him, as from the wild Indians, the narcs, and (in dream No. 5) the police. (Whether this represents fear of retaliation for his own acquisitiveness and, hence, projection of his own urges, is a possibility. But it also may indicate a primary distrust in the reliability and predictability of others.)

Dream No. 5. Policemen with guns and the need to run away constitute a familiar theme in this dream sequence.

The wish to have a girl seek him out sexually (a wish to be provided for with minimal effort on his part) is familiar. Covering up his real intentions or feelings (in this dream, from the girl's mother) has occurred in previous dreams.

The wish to dramatize himself and be exhibitionistic (as if on stage) has only been barely suggested in previous dreams. It jibes with his serious interest in being a movie director.

Motive No. 1. Wish to discontinue his college education and get a job.

Motive No. 2. Fear of severe punishment for his unacceptable urges.

Motive No. 3. Wish for free food, free sex, and free marihuana, that is, without any obligation.

Motive No. 4. Wish for companionship with others, especially men, to share his pleasures and punishments.

Motive No. 5. Fear of people stealing his possessions.

Motive No. 6. Need to cover up his motives or feelings, especially from father and mother figures.

Motive No. 7. Wish to show off or dramatize self or be recognized publicly.

56

Current Psychological Conflicts

The dreamer wants to discontinue his college education and get a job but he fears his father will disapprove. His own conscience gives him a much tougher time on this issue than his father, for in his dreams he fancies himself being hunted down and in danger of being killed by Indians or policemen. (This is a manifestation of his super ego.)

Underlying his wish to quit college and take a job is a more child-like motivation to be taken care of like a little child who gets many goodies free or with very little expenditure of effort. He is ashamed of these aspects of his plan to quit school, and he prefers to keep these hidden. Also, he has a guilty conscience about these urges to be dependent and to have all his wants be taken care of, and he fears and expects physical punishment just for thinking and dreaming about these desires.

Somehow in the dilemma of these conflicting aims, the dreamer is able to draw on some unknown personality resources and add a touch of humor, even slapstick comedy, to these situations. For this shy, reserved, and lonely young man, who aspires to be a playwright or a movie director, he lessens the severity of his conflicts by giving himself some companionship in his dreams and playing with the idea that maybe the dreams are only play-acting instead of the real thing.

Lifetime Psychological Conflicts

Without some data about the dreamer's life history and some free-associations we will not be able to document how long standing are some of the conflicts and coping mechanisms that have been discussed under *Current Psychological Conflicts*. We can be sure, however, that there must be a past history to some of the recurring behaviors pictured in the dreams. It is a safe guess that high standards for achievement were set for him by his parents, (and, hence, he has a strict conscience with respect to achieving goals once set), that he was well indulged and taken care of as a child (and, hence, longs to recapture this childhood paradise of plenty without effort), and that he has been a person who typically covers up his true feelings.

Shame and guilt feelings at not achieving academic or other goals must be long-standing psychological conflicts for this dreamer.

Example II

I have just presented one dream series (Example I) without free-associations but with a dream stimulus which required a lot of work towards analyzing the *current* and *lifetime* psychological conflicts underlying the dreams. The second dream series (Example II) includes rather detailed free-associations by a dreamer who was well acquainted with dream analysis, and he was able to save our energies in analyzing the psychological problems with which his dreams were dealing. Studying the second dream series carefully a reader may observe details and common elements that the dreamer ignored or, at least, did not mention. These might well constitute other valid clues and leads as to the personal meanings of this dream series that have not been touched on in the text. Single dreams and dream series are usually like this, one might say like poetry or some beautiful aspect of Nature, in that new discoveries and viewpoints keep turning up on reconsidering them and with further reflection. We will have to remind ourselves that this dreamer's free-associations are almost verbatim reports of the *spontaneous* unfolding of his own understanding of his dreams. As such, these are not final or complete formulations and interpretations of these dreams. Also, the dream stimuli for each of his dreams, though this is not spelled out in the following text, are usually the psychological experiences the dreamer was undergoing in each psychoanalytic session preceding his dream. We will see that there is a continuity to the inner problems he is coping with and with each dream a bit more information is added to our understanding of the kind of person he is and has been.

Furthermore, from this short fragment of a long psychoanalysis—which omits all the other important details of each psychoanalytic session except what pertains directly to the dreams—we can get a rough idea about the psychoanalytic procedure; especially the fact that the psychoanalytic patient re-experiences and relives with the psychoanalyst many forgotten past feelings about important relationships with members of the family from which one originated. This phenomenon is called the "transference neurosis," which means that old childhood emotions and experiences that one can hardly remember, but which nevertheless continue to influence one's present day-to-day reactions to oneself and others often in an inappropriate or irrational way (hence, called "neurosis"), are transferred (that is, relived and re-experienced) to the psychoanalyst in a situation of trust and contemplation where one can take a good look at oneself and these buried feelings. The reader should, hence, not be surprised that some of the dreams of this series contain, more than many we will review here, the person of the dreamer's psychoanalyst in disguised form. In this connection, it is not a simple matter to discern whether a dream character represents a projection of some portion of the personality of the dreamer or some individual entirely separate from the dreamer or both. But remember that when we dream (or for that matter think or feel some way about someone else) we are expressing our subjective reaction to someone else and this subjective reaction may not coincide exactly with external objects, but rather it may be distorted by our own faulty perceptions, memories, preconceptions, or stereotypes. So even when the characters in our dreams do represent primarily someone other than ourselves, these representations do include some coloring from our own personalities. Psychoanalysis tries to make the patient aware of the extent to which and the ways in which these misperceptions and distortions of others (and oneself) occur; and the phenomenon of the "transference neurosis" in psychoanalysis and the focussing of these various emotions and attitudes on the psychoanalyst is one of the means whereby the patient is helped to recalibrate his inner world, stemming from childhood impressions, with different individuals and life situations as they exist in the here-and-now.

The following series of dreams occurred near the termination of a lengthy didactic psychoanalysis of a psychiatrist who was in training to become a psychoanalyst. He was the father of two children, and his wife was about to have another child. A very perceptive and intelligent person, his own free-associations made dream analysis and interpretation relatively easy.

Dream No. 1. "I was standing in front of a glass door with a curtain in front of it. I pulled the curtain aside, and there was President Kennedy on the telephone. Another sound of some sort occurred, and he looked around to see what was the disturbing sound. I wanted to see that he wasn't disturbed."

"Then the scene changed to a bathroom scene. A green roach came in and I killed it. Another one came from under the wash basin, and I killed it, too. There was a furry animal nearby. I was afraid that by hitting the roaches I might hit this animal, too, and I didn't want to."

Free-Associations. "After having the dream, I recalled you said last time I must have some repressed feelings about the birth of my younger brother and sister. The dream expresses the emotional reactions to them that I repressed a long time ago. I must have experienced them as little pests (roaches) that I wanted to be rid of."

"The furry animal could represent my mother. One of the roaches was on the body of the furry animal. I had mixed feelings about hitting and hurting the animal—I thought I might have to in order to kill the roaches, but I wanted to avoid hitting the animal if I could. I guess I had mixed feelings (love and hate) toward my mother over these matters."

"President Kennedy was disturbed by at least one of the roaches. He represents the great father—me—disturbed by some annoying sound. I had the dream this morning after

I got up to look after one of my children who was crying; after tending to the child, I went back to sleep."

"Why were the cockroaches green? I've never seen one like that. This office is green. Also, green could represent envy and jealousy, but why were the roaches green and not I? Maybe to disown my own jealousy and attribute it to someone else (displacement)."

"I am reminded of my friend, Bill, who annoyed me yesterday by the manner in which he asked me to return a memo to him. I think of this, now, I believe because of my rivalry with him, although we work well together in our business partnership. He is a brother-figure for me, no doubt."

Dream No. 2. "I crashed into a red auto. A third auto was hit and turned over."

Free-Associations. "The dream shows my angry reaction to Bill. He shut me up when I was needling him about his religious ties, and said I should spend more time on our joint business matters."

"I guess I'd rather dwell on his impatience with me than on the fact that I provoked his reaction to me."

"Bill doesn't have a red car, but I think I made his car red because of the heat he can make me feel, for which I blame him."

Dream No. 3. "I was with a blond Russian girl. I was trying to hide from her the fact that I was married. Also, I was trying to keep my mother-in-law from seeing her. Also, I was hiding the fact that I was Jewish."

Free-Association. "I've expressed my affectionate feelings towards you before in my dreams in the guise of interest in a woman. This dream reveals my wish to preserve and hide my affectionate feelings toward you. The question is why should my affectionate feelings be portrayed in my dream as illicit or forbidden? Probably because a Jew is not supposed to like a non-Jew and vice versa. You're not blond, Russian, or a woman. I think those qualities add up to tender, intimate, nonhomosexual feelings for foreigners."

61

"When people would say, 'You don't look Jewish,' it would irritate me. I felt it was a qualified acceptance. However, I did prefer not to look Jewish—Semitic and Arabic people look similar. I think there's survival value in not looking Jewish."

"I expected my psychoanalysis to be completely intellectual—one in which I developed no transference neurosis (that is, emotional ties and neurotic reactions to the psychoanalyst). I thought the analysis would deal with basic drives and not with Jewish and non-Jewish issues."

"No, I realize behind these superficial concerns of mine is the basic issue or drive of how much am I loved."

*Dream No. 4a.** "I was driving a car. I had a map. Somebody said that we'd have to drive through Georgia."

Free Associations. "I think of Georgia as a southern state where there is a fair amount of prejudice against the Blacks. I think of it as populated with many narrow-minded people. I don't want to be associated with such people. Someone might raise the question whether I have prejudices, that I think I am better than others or belong to the chosen people. This is a topic I don't feel like I want to get into. In this connection, the dream may be dealing with my analysis and my wish to avoid certain topics because I have an idea that I'll stir up a lot of emotions in myself. That is, I have a map, and I know that going through Georgia is going to lead me into some unpleasant topics."

*Dream No. 4b.** "A travel service was trying to hire my secretary and give her a better job. I was annoyed at the travel service for doing this."

Free Associations. "My secretary asked me a question about one of my patients, and I thought her question was impertinent and none of her business; so I walked away from her without answering. I guess the dream was partly a reaction to this experience with my secretary. I suppose I was

---

*These dreams are labelled 4a and 4b because they were dreamt on the same night.

62

afraid she would be offered a job by someone else; my annoyance with the travel service in the dream tells me I wasn't hoping to get rid of her. She's a good secretary; Gad! I wonder whether my secretary in the dream also represents you. Am I afraid I'll lose you if I don't tell all! Could be!"

"Why should a travel service come into the dream scene and story? Maybe that's a continuation of the theme of where am I traveling at this point of my analysis? I don't seem to be enthusiastic about going to Georgia—that is, going into my prejudices that I am very special and that I hate to share somebody's attention with others."

Dream No. 5. "There wasn't much to this dream. There was a farm scene with arable acreage and a smaller, wooded, uncleared portion. I was just looking around this land."

Free-Associations. "The dream relates to my analysis. The wooded, uncleared portion is the unanalyzed part of my self. What I am missing is a clearer experience of pain with separation. I am going to miss some analytic hours at the end of this month. I am somewhat bothered that not everything has been analyzed, but I am not so perfectionistic about having every single conflict analyzed."

"I didn't work out all my Oedipal conflicts (romantic urges to steal his mother's love away from his father) in this psychoanalysis by having fantasies about your wife. She's blond. I had more fantasies about Catherine, a dark-haired woman, whose hair was similar in color to my mother's."

Dream No. 6. "I was in a semi-dark anteroom adjoining another room. A bright yellow cat was in front of the door. The cat wanted to get into the other room. I went to do just that for it. The cat was very angry and talked about being neglected. He said he'd been excluded, and he was angry because I hadn't let him into the next room."

Free-Associations. "The yellow color reminds me of a yellow Star of David. The cat is I. It is a humiliated animal that is enraged! Very early in my analysis I had a dream about an angry lion. The analysis has reduced my rage from a lion's to a cat's. There's still some anger there."

"Another meaning of yellow in the United States is cowardice. But in the country where I grew up yellow was more often associated with envy. There are frequent sentences in novels to the effect that the yellow envy had almost eaten him up."

"I was surprised in the dream that the cat would express a minor slight so intensely. All I had done was walk into the middle of the room and then away from the cat before letting him out of the room."

"I suspect this relates to my irritation at having to wait several months before I was able to get started in analysis with you."

"Actually, I had selected two more prominent training analysts, before I settled on you. My first two choices were based on my narcissism. Seeking a psychoanalysis with you, when I reflect on it now, was on a more fundamental and mature basis."

Common Themes. The themes of envy, jealousy, possessiveness, and resentment recur through these dreams, involving his brother and sister, his own offspring, his father, the psychoanalyst. Shame and guilt over unacceptable impulses appear to be the principal components leading to conflicts over these emotions.

Motive No. 1. (dream No. 1) Anger and jealousy over attention and recognition mothers give to (other) children which conflicts with guilt and shame.

Wish to be a great and important person.

Motive No. 2. (dream No. 2) Need to express anger to friends (brother figures) who challenge him which conflicts with fear he may be injured too if he lets go.

Motive No. 3. (dream No. 3) Preoccupation with wooing some forbidden woman (the analyst, as a mother-figure, or the analyst's wife, as an Oedipal figure) and these motivations make him feel ashamed and guilty.

Motive No. 4. (dreams No. 4a and 4b) Wish not to face his overevaluation of himself and his reluctance to sharing dependent support and recognition.

Motive No. 5. (dream No. 5) Wish to perceive and know the extent of his self-understanding and his unanalyzed self.

Motive No. 6. (dream No. 6) Need to understand precisely how he becomes resentful if his wants or desires are delayed by others.

Current Psychological Conflicts

The dreamer is reliving in the present and in the psychoanalytic situation with his analyst a lifetime of sibling rivalry, competition for a mother's attention, uncontrollable rage at the frustration of immediate satisfaction of his desires, and the embarrassment, shame, and guilt that made many of these feelings inaccessible to his consciousness.

Lifetime Psychological Conflicts

This dreamer's confident pride and self-assurance must have been instilled early in his upbringing through love and indoctrination by his family. These serve him well in adversity and have survival value. His bitter sibling rivalry and possessiveness of mother figures interfere with his capacity to love generously those who are dependent on him and inhibit his realizing his optimal creative potentials.

In the formulation of the *current psychological conflicts* and *lifetime psychological conflicts* of this dreamer, I have summarized these rather than spell out in much more detail what might be said. With this dream series, I primarily want the reader to perceive the richness of the dreamer's free-associations towards understanding the psychodynamics behind his dreams. One can notice that even with his free-associations, being unusually informative with respect to the psychodynamic meanings behind the dream scene, characters, or action, that initial conclusions about the significance of a dream certainly do not reveal the whole story. Later dreams and free-associations cast a clearer light on some implications

65

in earlier dreams that were not initially apparent or convincing. A good example of this, and, incidentally, also of the concept of overdetermination in dreams (many simultaneously different meanings), is dream No. 3 about "a blond, Russian woman" with whom the dreamer was obviously being seductive. From his associations on the day he reported this dream one can be perhaps surprised but satisfied that the "blond, Russian girl" represents the analyst (who is not blond nor of Russian background) and the dreamer's wish to attract the attention, recognition, and love of the analyst as the dreamer successfully attracted his mother (who was dark-haired and not Russian). But in the associations to dream No. 5 we learn that the dreamer is aware of certain unanalyzed portions of his personality, one of which includes his romantic fantasies about taking his mother away from his father. In this connection, he casually mentions he has noticed the analyst's *blond* wife, but hastens to lead us to believe that she was not the "blond Russian girl" in dream No. 3 by confessing he has been more attracted to a dark-haired married woman. Even with initial denials of this sort by the most astute dream analyst, we should maintain some continuing skepticism that there is more to the first interpretation than meets the eye. In other words, a certain tentativeness should be maintained that all the connections and complexities of a dream have been ascertained after the first few considerations.

Example III

The next example of a dream series is taken from a psychotherapist's notes of a patient whose therapy was being terminated because the therapist was moving to a different city. In this dream series, we have the stimulus for the dream series, the dreams, the free-associations, and the interpretative comments of the psychotherapist, which sometimes seem to simply repeat the gist of what the dreamer has already said about his dream and on other occasions which definitely add another helpful interpretive point of view. The dreams in this series occurred over a two-week period.

The dreamer was a happily married man with three children who had already been receiving psychoanalytic psychotherapy for over a year when the therapist announced he was going to be leaving the city in three months and the psychotherapeutic relationship would have to soon come to an end. The option of continuing therapy with another therapist or discontinuing psychotherapy permanently had been tentatively discussed at the time these dreams were reported. The patient's original symptoms which had brought him into treatment had long been relieved, and though the original complaints of some patients not infrequently temporarily recur as the termination of psychotherapy is being discussed, this patient had consciously experienced no such problems.

Dream Series Stimulus. The psychotherapist had told the patient a month previously that the psychotherapy would stop in two months and that he was moving to a distant city in three months.

Dream No. 1. "I alternated between being a child and an adult. Often I was a child, about a 10-year-old, observing myself as an adult."

"In one scene, I was with a bunch of boys who were going fishing. I wanted to get in line to go on this fishing trip; I jumped in front of someone in line. That's all I can remember of the dream."

Free-Associations. "I guess I wish to get in front of someone in line. This suggests I want somebody's position. I don't fish very often. In fact, I'm really not much of a fisherman. The act of fishing reminds me of dredging up something from the depths, say from my unconscious. Fishing has an element of luck in it, like the grab bag they used to have in candy stores. I suppose the dream indicates I want to get ahead of somebody in line to catch a surprise or obtain some food."

*("The early part of the dream helps us date the period in your life when you were first experiencing the psychological state with which the dream process is dealing. Apparently, something happening here and involving our work together or something elsewhere in your life has reminded you of some life experiences when you were about 10 years of age. We could say the 10-year-old boy in you is surveying your present-life situation and decides that breaking into a waiting line of boys to go fishing may offer some solution for what ails you.")

"I have been thinking of finishing my psychotherapy here with you. That's a little more then one month away now. I feel good about myself and the progress and recovery I have made from the problems and symptoms I originally came to see you about. As I look at myself now, I think I've come a long, long way from my boyhood worries. My work is going very well. I don't think I need to get in therapy with someone else after you leave."

"But the thought did cross my mind whether I always want to stay in this city here or go to the beautiful part of the U.S. where you are moving."

("Sounds like, in your dream, the secret thought was to come along with me, but you didn't want to put it so openly. Instead, you changed that idea into sneaking in line to go on a fishing trip and left the reason why and with whom very vague.")

Dream No. 2. "My wife went riding in a sky balloon with a man, his wife, and two young children. I didn't quite understand the arrangement. She said they threw cherry bombs from the balloon that would ricochet off things and explode. Someone showed me pictures of the balloon. The man sometimes had a beard or glasses. Over water the balloon pulled people on water skis or under water. I worried

---

*Paragraphs in parentheses signify psychotherapist's remarks to the dreamer or unexpressed thoughts of the therapist about the dreamer and his associations.

68

how safe the tow rope was. It could break. I snapped it and broke it. My wife said it wasn't getting snapped. It was only being used for snapping."

Free-Associations. "My wife and I have only two children at home. The rest are away on vacation. My wife and I quarreled and we slept in separate beds last night. We had some house guests and they spent a lot of time quarreling, which helped produce our quarreling. I think I am having a reaction to the coming termination of my psychotherapy. My wife thinks I am more isolated and keep to myself. I haven't noticed this or any other symptom. Maybe I do behave differently. My wife says I am controlling. I complain she doesn't contribute to my decisions and then she complains about the ones I make. She complains about kids at home and the problems there."

"The man in the balloon—I am not sure why he had a beard sometimes and sometimes glasses. I've seen pictures of Sigmund Freud with and without a beard and with and without glasses. The man, in some remote way, may represent you or the psychotherapy. You, of course, don't have a beard, but sometimes you wear glasses and you are a psychotherapist. The balloonist had his wife and two children aboard; that could be a mirror-image of my wife and two children at home, that is, I could be giving my wife and two children to the balloonist for some reason, like making you and me identical twins with the same wife and the same two children I have. That could be one way of keeping most of my family together with you. The only person I have left out is myself. The fact that the sky balloon dangles a tow rope out of the basket to pull a water skier or somebody under the water would be one way to keep me along with the group. Since I had quarreled with my wife and our psychotherapy is coming to a close I can't let myself be aboard, but I want to have some kind of connection with the group. That may be why I am so preoccupied with the security of the connection between the balloon and the person being towed. Obviously, the fact that the tow rope can break when you snap it reveals that I am worried that the umbilical cord or other connections between people can be broken. The part of the dream where my wife says the tow was only being used for snapping is puzzling to me. I suspect that means that the connections between people can be used for holding them together and can be used for snapping at or fighting with each other. The cherry bombs exploding and so forth, that suggests some kind of anger at work, maybe the fireworks between my wife and me."

(The dreamer did not free-associate on the details that he saw pictures of the balloon; dreaming of seeing pictures or dreaming that one is dreaming puts distance between the dreamer and the feelings and experiences being visualized, and this can be a mechanism of defense against experiencing certain feelings too strongly.)

Dream No. 3. "I had just finished college. I went to an old warehouse and there were two entrances to the building. To get where I wanted to go in the warehouse I had to go through somebody else's quarters, and I was embarrassed. The warehouse was only one-half full of whatever I was going to sell—food or groceries I think. I asked someone to send me some wrappers to wrap the product. I remained embarrassed going through the other person's property. I came back to the warehouse and I found that I didn't have much stock left in the warehouse. I couldn't figure out what had happened to my stock. I figured I should take inventory and maybe I would find some more valuable products. Or, maybe I was bankrupt."

Free-Associations. "I awakened from this dream very depressed. The warehouse with the two entrances was my unconscious. The inventory was my psychotherapy. I guess I'm re-experiencing the sadness I felt on graduating from college."

("Apparently you feel threatened in the loss of supplies of attention and support you will lose by the termination of this psychotherapy. You equate that with loss of food stores" [symbolization].)

70

"That probably is so. Then, the embarrassment I felt in the dream about going through someone's quarters is my anxiety about revealing my dependency to someone else, namely, to you and myself."

("Yes, and trying to find some material to wrap the product is trying to find a way to hide it from public view.")

"Yes. And I felt in the dream that maybe someone had stolen these supplies from me. And whatever had happened I might be destitute—just plain bankrupt!"

("Maybe we can now get a better perspective on the balloon dream you reported last session. That dream, as we suspected before, reveals your separation anxiety. Our plans to terminate our psychotherapeutic sessions plus your quarrel and night's separation from your wife aroused the memories of old separation fears. Besides the two offsprings you have at home, you know you had two brothers and in the dream process you seem to be separating not only from your wife, your two children, your psychotherapist, but also the symbolic representations of your mother, father, and two brothers.")

Dream No. 4. "I was driving a big tractor trailer and the rear axle cracked and went bad. I tried to patch it up until I got to the next stop."

Free-Associations. "The feelings I had in the dream was one of great frustration and despair. The tractor was a good one and very powerful. I know in previous dreams that the car or truck I am driving in the dreams often represents my body and my personality, and the type of car I am driving and what happens in the dream demonstrates what I am thinking about my strengths and my weaknesses and what I hope for or fear. In the present dream, I am pleased that the tractor-trailer is pictured as a big and powerful one; I suspect the trailer part of the vehicle is the family I have fathered and must provide for. But why I have the rear axle go bad, I can't imagine."

("I think you are feeling that I am your rear axle and

71

that I am giving out on you in our plan to terminate your psychotherapy.")

Dream No. 5. "I was in a track meet. The timekeeper said that so-and-so ran the race in 61 seconds. I knew it couldn't have been done in that amount of time."

Free-Associations. "I knew, in the dream, that it was impossible for anyone to finish such a race in so short a time. Yet the timekeeper said that the guy who won the race had finished it in a phenomenally short time. If this dream has something to do with my psychotherapy, I suppose it reveals my skepticism that there has been enough time to do the job, travel the distance so to speak, that is really required."

("Yes, I think you are indicating in this dream that more time is necessary to complete the task of psychotherapy properly. It's curious, though, that you come to realize this fact in the context of a competitive race. Have you been aware that you have been comparing yourself with others in this matter of how long psychotherapy should last and that you have wanted to try to beat out others on this score?")

Dream No. 6. "My wife and I were going to New York City. There were several sequences in which we were disappointed. I can't remember all of them. In one, we went to a restaurant and the service and everything else was poor. In another, I broke into a store and stole some things and throughout this burglary scene I felt I was being watched, and I felt quite guilty."

Free-Associations. "Although I don't consciously feel nearly so deprived and unhappy as I seemed to be in this dream, I get the message that I am experiencing this relationship with you as if starvation were just around the corner. And if I am going to make ends meet and take care of my addiction to you, I am going to have to go out and steal. It is amazing to me that I am making such a big fuss of the termination of our work together. This whole situation is affecting some sensitive nerve that I haven't been aware of or ever knew existed. I remember now that mother used to have to join dad sometimes in the evenings and help with the inven-

72

tory-taking in the family business. I was usually left without a sitter, and if I cried, mother would say I shouldn't because I was big enough to take care of myself and that she wasn't far away. My older brother was usually helping them, and I had the job—in addition to looking after myself—of being responsible for my little brother."

("You had too much responsibility too early for child care, including looking after yourself, and you really had something to feel deprived about in those days.")

"Yes, I remember I often tried to steal out of the house when I was left there with my brother, and when he was asleep, and I'd try to join my parents. They thought it was funny the first couple of times, but after that they scolded me and wouldn't permit me to come along."

Common Themes and Motives

Dream No. 1. Motive No. 1. The dreamer, regressing to the age of a 10-year-old boy, wishes to sneak along on a (fishing) trip with the psychotherapist.

Motive No. 2. The dreamer, as an adult, is unaware of wanting to accompany the therapist after termination of the therapy or if he is, he is too embarrassed about this urge to acknowledge it openly.

Dream No. 2. Motive No. 3. The theme appears of putting distance between people and Mother Earth and himself (by his wife and a representation of his therapist being carried off the earth in an air balloon).

Motive No. 4. A preoccupation with the potential fragility of ties between people appears.

Motive No. 5. With the issue of fishing in Dream No. 1 and water skiing or being pulled under water in Dream No. 2, the symbolization of water is presented. In the context of this dream series, the idea of delving under the surface of one's personality for more information about his reactions is suggested. Also, suggested is a wish to return to life in the womb, that is, to a position of such safety and security, in view of the impending separation from the therapist and the

73

night's separation from his wife. But this idea is admittedly more speculative.

Dream No. 3. Motive No. 6. Fear of depletion of his food supplies (symbolizing security, support, and love) which conflicts with shame and embarrassment at this anxiety being discovered by others.

Dream No. 4. Motive No. 7. Fear of breakdown of his power to pull weight of his responsibilities if psychotherapist stops seeing him.

(In this connection, the fact that the therapist always sat behind the patient while he lay on a couch, and in the dream it was his tractor's rear axle that gave out illustrates the dream processes of *symbolization, condensation,* and *displacement.* The dreamer is equating the psychotherapist, who sits behind him, with the rear axle of his tractor and, by extension, with his own virility.)

Dream No. 5. Motive No. 8. Fear that he has to carry out an almost impossible race with time to achieve his goals.

Dream No. 6. Motive No. 9. Fear of starvation to the point where he must steal which, in turn, makes him feel guilty.

Current Psychological Conflicts

The dreamer is experiencing increasing separation anxiety, fear of desertion, and helplessness at the prospect of termination of his psychotherapy. One of the remedies he conceives of, in this situation which seems so urgent to him, is to steal some supplies (of confidence, self-esteem, external support) and this plagues him with a sense of guilt.

Lifetime Psychological Conflicts

A deep, not previously apparent, psychological conflict is aroused by the termination phase of this dreamer's psychotherapy. The current psychological conflicts that are evoked by this situation have their origins in the dreamer's boyhood, when his parents periodically left him alone at night at home in charge of a younger brother. If he cried about his separation anxiety and his sense of being given excessive responsibility, he was put to shame by his parents for crying. If he stole out of his house to try to join his parents, he was scolded and made to feel guilty. These old, incompletely resolved childhood conflicts are the sources of the strong emotions which emerge in the contents of his dreams under the circumstances of the discontinuation of his psychotherapy.

Chapter V

RECURRENT DREAMS

Some people have recurrent dreams; that is, dreams that have exactly the same or similar themes and that are dreamt repeatedly. These repetitive dreams are common in childhood, but adults not infrequently report having dreams of this sort, too.

Do these repetitive dreams have different biological and psychological bases than the dreams that have been described thus far? Do these kinds of dreams signify something different from dreams in which the manifest content or theme is not very similar to the themes of other dreams?

Repetitive dreams are like nonrepetitive dreams with respect to their biological and psychodynamic bases. But they are different in that the psychological conflicts leading to the dream theme are not changed by having the dream itself or by intervening waking events, for example, psychotherapy or good fortune, that might otherwise help resolve the oppressive psychological dilemmas that are contributing to the dream story or dream content. That is, the dreamer is continuing to be faced with the same urges and goals and anxieties associated with these drives and has developed no new ways of dealing with them. There may be several reasons why the dreamer has not increased his skills or abilities to modify or improve his ways of dealing with these psychological conflicts:

1. *The dreamer is simply not aware of the nature of the inner psychological conflicts producing the dream story and, hence, is unable to work on trying out different solutions to these personal problems.*

2. *The dreamer has some inkling of the psychological conflicts which are bothering him, but does not know what to do about the conflicts or how to change his approach to them.*

Young children are often in this situation because they have relatively little say-so over the rules and regulations which affect their daily lives, but rather they are subject to their parents' control. Moreover, their range of coping mechanisms in the ordinary problems of living are limited; for example, problems in the areas of impulse versus control, independence versus dependence, trust versus distrust, and so forth. For various reasons, adults are sometimes in life situations which they cannot change or avoid and these situations trigger or expose them to problems they cannot readily solve, for example, sexual temptations, fear of desertion or withdrawal of support, or unescapable pressures against the expression of anger or rage.

3. *The emotions aroused by some life event or events are so overwhelming or catastrophic that the memories associated with the experience are indelibly etched in one's mind, and they may return to haunt the dreamer at even slight provocations.*

The dreamer is easily reminded by everyday events, during wakefulness, of this catastrophe, which may include the death of a loved one or a threat to one's continued existence. Since the range of effective psychological coping mechanisms with such situations is limited and lies more in the direction of passive resignation and mourning rather than active mastering and overcoming, dreaming about such events is not likely to have much variation in theme.

Nonrepetitive dreams, on the other hand, usually do not have these background characteristics. Let me give some examples of repetitive dreams to illustrate these features.

Example I

A mother's little four-year-old boy developed a fatal kidney disease. He seemed to be responding, briefly, to hospital treatment, but one day when the mother went to the hospital to visit her little son, she found him lying in bed dead. She picked up his body and held it close to her to try to revive him, though the physician-in-charge had already declared him dead and signed the death certificate. She refused to surrender the boy's body and cried loudly and endlessly. Finally, she was persuaded by her husband to give up her son's body and leave the hospital.

As a result of this experience, she had a nervous breakdown, characterized by unconsolable grief, that required a period of treatment in a mental hospital. On discharge from the hospital and periodically for more than ten years thereafter, she had vivid nightmares with the following theme.

Recurrent Dream No. 1: She clearly saw her son lying dead in bed exactly as she had seen him the day she went to the hospital and found him so. There was no other action or scene in this vivid dream. She was definitely the person looking at the dead boy. She felt a painful sense of loss and intense grief overwhelm her as she gazed at the child. The dream invariably awakened her in a fit of crying.

This example particularly illustrates item No. 3 above, namely, the potential of a catastrophic event, that one has no easy method of handling psychologically, to trigger recurrent dreams. Recurring threats to one's own life, prisoner of war or refugee camp experiences, and so forth, can precipitate the occurrence of repetitive dreams in certain individuals.

The mother who lost her toddler son tried to handle her recurring nightmare by staying up all night and not sleeping and taking light naps during the day. When this did not absolutely prevent her dreaming, she began taking whatever varieties of psychomotor stimulant drugs she could get from several different physicians or over-the-counter at her neighborhood drug store so that she could stay awake several days at a time, and then take several sleeping pills to try to sleep so deeply she would not dream. This approach did not work to her advantage either, for she still occasionally had her nightmare. In this connection, there is evidence that nightmares often occur during the fourth stage of sleep, rather than during rapid eye movement (REM), stage two sleep. This poor mother finally got relief from her repetitive nightmare through psychotherapy designed to help her more effectively complete her mourning and give up her attachment to her son who had died so many years ago. Recently, scientists have learned that certain types of minor tranquilizers called "benzodiazepines" specifically suppress stage four sleep and may, hence, be helpful in relieving the victims of nightmares, whether or not the nightmares are repetitive in theme. The use of such pharmacologic agents by themselves may assist in suppressing the occurrence of a nightmare, but will have no favorable influence on the dreamer's psychological need to have dreams with such themes in the first place. At this time in our knowledge, only psychotherapy suffices to remedy the underlying mental depression resulting from a grief reaction.

Example II

A college student reported the following dream which had occurred repeatedly over many years.

Recurrent Dream No. 2: "I am being flown in an airplane and the person flying the plane is unknown to me, and the whole experience is very frightening to me."

The only comment that the student had to offer that might serve as a clue related to the historical background of this recurrent dream was that her parents had separated when she was ten years of age and they had soon thereafter been divorced. Sometimes, several years before and after this period of her life, she lived for brief occasions with her maternal grandmother or a paternal aunt and uncle instead of with either parent.

The manifest dream content puts the patient in a situation far off the ground which is not itself considered perilous during this age of airline travel. It does symbolize, however, considerable distance from the relative safety of having one's "feet-on-the-ground" and being close to so-called "mother earth." The flying position, on the other hand, could be exciting or exhilarating, as it often is meant to be in dreams symbolizing sexual desire and stimulation or the enjoyable feelings associated with newly developed ability to be independent or the mastery of some difficult problem. But our dreamer experiences this dream as a frightening one with the implications that one could fall from a great height and be hurt, a common emotional reaction embedded in the kind of anxiety psychiatrists refer to as "separation anxiety," an overly strong fear concerning real or imagined threat of loss of support or love from someone upon whom one customarily relies.

The uncertainty about who is piloting the plane makes the dream situation even more precarious, and corroborates the idea that the dreamer keeps being preoccupied with whose hands she is in now and what is the identity and the nature of the commitment of the person entrusted with the guardianship of her life and fate?

We can, with reasonable assurance, surmise the following psychological conflicts underlying this recurrent dream.

Current Psychological Conflict

An event has recently occurred which makes her think of being independent and self-sufficient, but because she feels she lacks the know-how to manage this confidently herself, she passively puts herself in the care of or under the guidance of someone else. The identity and reliability of the person she depends on always seems to be in question and this makes her fearful of being misled or dropped .

Long-term Psychological Conflict

The childhood distress she suffered with respect to who was going to be responsible for parenting her, with her real parents quarreling and separating, has left an indelible worry in her mind. Children at the age of ten or younger often wish they could be on their own and manage without relying on parental rule or whim but they invariably discover that the complexities of life, especially in our society, make them ill-equipped to make it on their own. Hence, they are obliged to be dependent on whoever will take responsibility for them.

This recurrent dream tells us that the dreamer experienced insecurity and repeated separation anxiety as a child as to who would be her parent or parental substitute. As a young adult, she is unconsciously reminded of this childhood dilemma, and she has this recurrent dream, whenever new steps toward independent thinking or action have to be taken or whenever someone seems to threaten her normal needs for support or love.

Example III

Another college student had a recurrent dream very similar in manifest content to the one described in Example II. The recurring dream differed from Example II in that it gradually changed in certain important details of its content over the years and became significantly less frightening.

Recurrent Dream No. 3: "I was in an airplane, always as a passenger, and I would never know who was the pilot. The plane would nose-dive and be about to crash. I would always wake up before it crashed.

"Each time I had the dream I moved up among the passenger seats towards the pilot. Recently, on two occasions, I was the co-pilot of the plane. The very last time I had the dream, I was the pilot. The nose-diving of the plane has been under control, and there has not been much threat of crashing."

Free-Associations. Unfortunately, no free-associations on this recurrent dream were available. The dreamer did, however, say that this recurrent dream had not been dreamt for several years.

Long-term Psychological Conflict

We can only guess that this student had some life circumstances similar to the student who had recurrent dream No. 2. We cannot be certain about exactly what life experiences resulted in this dreamer's being very wary of dependence and especially biased that the person on whom dependence was placed would be an unreliable and destructive person.

The *old psychological conflict* depicted by the initial form of the recurrent dream was: A need or wish to be dependent on someone which conflicted with the fear that the would-be supporting figure would prove untrustworthy and threatening to one's survival.

Current Psychological Conflict

Dream stimuli: Some life events must have been occurring which have made the dreamer obliged to consider relying or being dependent on another human being. Normal human relationships, which require being able to love and to work, necessitate the ability to feel secure whenever one depends on other people.

The more current psychological conflict in this recurrent dream originates from the older psychological conflict. What is interesting to see, in the evolution of this recurrent dream, is how the dreamer finds a way to deal with the uncertainty of the situation, namely, by becoming closer and closer and finally actively involved in a collaborative way (co-pilot) with the pilot. Developing the confidence of being able to manage to fly the plane oneself (take care of one's life affairs), also has helped the dreamer overcome deep anxieties.

This dreamer has, apparently, grown up and overcome deep doubts and anxieties about reliance on others and oneself. Recurrent dreams usually stop occurring with such emotional development and maturation. Apparently, the dreamer has stopped having this dream.

Example IV

Another student provided this example of a recurring dream. Again, the circumstances under which this dream was obtained were such that no additional clues were available from free-association to help specifically clarify the dream stimuli and the originating and precipitating life experiences leading to the dream work behind this dream theme. We will have to work back ourselves to try to fill in the blanks. This can be an extremely enlightening process that can sometimes give us amazing insights about the psychological processes of others and ourselves. We should always conscientiously remind ourselves, however, when indulging in this kind of guesswork—a very first step in every legitimate scientific research effort—that more corroborative data should always be sought and that our hypotheses should be altered to fit facts rather than changing facts to fit our hypotheses.

Recurrent Dream No. 4: "I was in my mother's house. All of a sudden the house started shaking, and I ran. I was running across an open field. I met a girl friend. The earth was now shaking very badly. The earth opened up on one side of me. Behind me flames and rocks shot up out of the ground. I made my way hurriedly up some nearby mountains and that turned out to be the safest place."

Hypothetical reconstruction of the missing parts of a recurrent dream

Without first-hand data from the dreamer, a young woman, the dream analyst has to try to reconstruct the dream elements empathically from his or her own life experiences and supply knowledge he has about the dream work (*symbolization, condensation,* and *displacement*) and from understandings of psychological defense and coping mechanisms.

A small group of similar high school students, who were

presented this problem in dream analysis, came up with the following ideas about this recurrent dream:

Old or long-term psychological conflict

This dream must have originally occurred in reaction to the fear that some world-shaking, violent, destructive event might take place that could swallow up ("the earth opened up . . .") or kill many people, including the dreamer's mother, girl friend, and self.

The event could be an explosive release of the dreamer's pent-up feelings, of passionate proportions, that somehow involve the dreamer's mother and a girl friend. If this is so, the dreamer must believe that these passions, originating from hidden unconscious sources within herself (from deep down under the earth), are dangerous. Hence, the dreamer must disapprove of these strong emotions of hers. The basic conflict is thus: an urge to release powerful feelings involving mother, which conflicts with guilt, shame, and fear of injury.

The recurrent dream may have followed the experiencing of a real earthquake and may simply be a rerun of the fear mobilized by an earthquake. But if this is so, why does not everyone have such recurring dreams after being in an earthquake, granting that a small percentage of people do have such dreams after being in an earthquake? The answer to this important question is that those relatively few people who have recurring earthquake dreams after experiencing a real earthquake are very likely to have had personal psychological conflicts that lend themselves to earthquake symbolism, that is, must have been worrying about the eruption of world-shaking emotions, including possible consequences of experiencing such emotions.

If the dreamer has never been through an earthquake, the hypothesized psychological conflict is even more likely.

Current Psychological Conflict

The current psychological conflict behind such a recurrent dream must be: an impulse to express very strong feelings (probably involving a mother or a mother-figure) which conflicts with a fear of loss of control of these emotions due to internalized guilt, shame, or fear of hurting oneself and others).

Dream stimuli that could evoke such a recurrent dream would be any experience (originating from external or internal sources) that might briefly upset the balance between the dreamer's impulsiveness and self-control.

Example V

Recurrent Dream No. 5 of floods, tidal waves, hurricanes, tornadoes, volcanoes and so forth: These have in common the unleashing of powerful natural forces which are outside of mankind's ability to harness or control. The symbolism behind such recurring dreams is similar to that behind earthquake dreams.

The perennial conflict of impulse versus self-discipline and control can be thought of as one of the basic personal conflicts behind such recurring dreams.

Example VI

A twenty-eight-year-old man reported that he had had the following recurring dream during his childhood. The dream had not occurred for about eight or nine years, but it had been dreamt several times a year from about the ages of six to twelve. He recalled that his grandfather had died just before these dreams started, and he had seen this relative in an open coffin at the mortuary. He was not allowed to go to the interment, but his mother told him about it. He remembered asking how can people breathe if buried? And he was told they did not breathe any more because they did not need air. For several years after this, he was afraid of sleeping in the dark and cried if he could not have a night light.

Recurrent Dream No. 6: "A black, steel gray cloud was always rolling after me. It was very scary. The dream was accompanied by a steel-gray, metallic taste in my mouth. The cloud never got me. It was always some distance behind me."

Free-Associations. The dreamer gave the following associations to this old, recurring dream. "The cloud had no structure. The thought I have about the gray-black cloud is that it represents a mood, a depressed mood I sometimes have. I used to have fears of dying by suffocation. As a kid I worried that if I did bad things or had sinful thoughts I could be punished by losing God's grace, and I would not go to Heaven. I was also taught that the Devil could take over one's soul. Since I was just like any other boy, and did the usual amount of mischief, you can imagine I had my share of scoldings and reprimands."

Motive No. 1. Childhood urges to be normally aggressive and mischievous.

Motive No. 2. Childhood religious and parental rearing giving him the concept that he could be influenced and possessed by evil and sinful spirits and urges.

Motive No. 3. Normal early childhood misconceptions and fears of darkness, dying, and death.

Initial dream stimulus. Death and funeral of grandparent.

Initial psychological conflct. (Ages six to eight.) Normal aggressive and sexual urges of boyhood which conflict with fears of losing control of these urges or, from his boyhood point of view, of being overwhelmed by mysterious, deadly evil spirits.

Later psychological conflict. (Ages ten to twelve.) The later developmental interactions of this conflict are: forbidden aggressive or sexual urges conflicting with guilty fear and shame, and these urges are seen by the dreamer, now, as being punishable by a depressive (gray-black) mood, a not uncommon consequence of the arousal of guilty fear and shame.

Chapter VI

LIMITATION IN THE ANALYSIS OF ONE'S DREAMS

Perhaps the most phenomenal example of the analysis of one's own dreams was Sigmund Freud's self-analysis. We learn that his analysis went on for many years, much of it documented in his correspondence with one of his best friends (Wilhelm Fliess) and in his publication *The Interpretation of Dreams*. The analysis of his own dreams was an important part of this self-psychoanalysis, which in fact led to many of the great discoveries about dream interpretation that have been described earlier in this book. Some of the pitfalls in the analysis of one's own dreams that Freud learned about are applicable to the self-analysis of dreams today. These obstacles rarely present themselves in any obvious way during the analysis of a few dreams. Rather, they begin to show up when one begins to fathom the depths of one's mind by continuing exploration and analysis of one's dreams.

I. *Some disturbing urges or impulses expressed in one's dreams, the dreamer does not want to know about.*

I believe that anyone selecting a book of this sort to read and study is motivated towards self-knowledge. But as one proceeds towards self-understanding, there are obstacles, internal ones, which hinder one's reaching such goals. These hindrances are acquired, learned sometime in our lifetime, and they tell us that we are bad or wicked or shameful or otherwise unlovable for having certain kinds of motivations

89

or desires. For many of us merely the thought or feeling of any one of these unacceptable wishes is the same as the deed, that is, as carrying out any action associated with the thought or urge. The Ten Commandments and the Seven Deadly Sins* include some of these forbidden attitudes or deeds.

These restrictive rules of human existence are indoctrinated in us by the people who care for us as we are growing up, and they become part of the code of ethics by which each individual regulates his thoughts and behaviors in our civilization. These rules of conduct that are so early and deeply embedded in us and are the products of our rearing before we were able to talk and, for some of us, for some years thereafter, form our unconscious conscience (Super Ego). Most of us do not know the extent and force of this very restrictive, self-punitive portion of our conscience. Our conscious conscience (Ego Ideal) also contains restrictive and inhibiting forces (Negative Ego Ideal), but our positive goals and aspirations can be classified as belonging to our Ego Ideal. Our unconscious conscience sets limits on how honestly and directly we can let ourselves see some of the more unacceptable drives in our dreams. This process of self-constraint in freely discovering and understanding oneself has been called "resistance" by psychoanalysts.

The clues that our unconscious conscience is at work setting limits on how far one can proceed with continuing self-analysis of dreams are usually not conscious thoughts that one should not proceed or that one is doing something evil or unforgivable. Rather, the clues are possibly moodiness, depression, growing lack of interest in this pursuit or perhaps a sense of fatigue or an idea that the whole enterprise is foolish or mystical and without validity. These are a few of the ways in which these unconscious deterrents to learning about oneself are manifested. Another, more difficult clue to deal with is that one may begin not to remember one's dreams,

---

*1. Vainglory, 2. Covetousness, 3. Lust, 4. Envy, 5. Gluttony, 6. Anger, 7. Sloth or Indolence.

which obviously brings the whole enterprise to a decisive halt.

Sometimes, some self-scrutiny into the strict no-no's that are part of one's code of behavior helps change the strength of this resistance. Or a self-reminder that thoughts and feeling are much different, in actuality and in their consequences, from actions and deeds may lessen this resistance. (For example, the wish that someone will drop dead is legally and actually much different than the deed, and everyone has had such ideas in a lifetime, with varying amounts of guilt and self-recrimination, of course.) Sometimes telling the dream to someone else interested in self-knowledge and dream analysis will provide some leads about the inhibiting and constraining motivations in the dream and, hence, in the dreamer. Another person, also interested in self-knowledge and dream analysis, may see the dream with a fresh viewpoint and can point out the self-punitive and self-restrictive aspects of the dream. For most of us, our unacceptable impulses towards others are accompanied by equally unkind impulses towards ourselves. Running away from self-realization of these urges in our dreams does not change us in any way; we will still behave the same ways towards others and ourselves. Delving into more self-understanding through our dreams, though this will not dramatically cure us of psychological conflicts bred in childhood, will move us in the directions of knowing ourselves better. I do not want to leave the reader with the impression that it is always safe and wise to turn to another person who has an amateur interest in dream analysis and enlist this person in serious analyzing and interpreting one's dreams. Truly expert assistance from others in such a project requires long and ethical professional training. The services of a psychoanalytically trained psychotherapist is the most effective measure towards eliminating blocks in self-analysis of one's dreams.

II. *Even though a dreamer is not blocked by an unconscious conscience (that dictates that knowing too much about oneself is dangerous), the dreamer lacks the knowledge about and experience with dreams that makes this approach easy or fruitful.*

Some people have a knack at self-inquiry and are quite psychologically-minded about themselves. Such people can make use of the ideas presented here and learn more about themselves. Some people are not very psychologically-minded though they may be brilliant in their vocations, the business world, in engineering, in the sciences, or the legal or medical professions. They tend to relate to others in terms of surface reactions or external appearance and are not inclined to look for underlying causes or why a person said or did such and such a thing. They tend to relate to their own selves in the same manner. Many individuals of this sort can improve their skills in understanding their own psychology. But many cannot. And they cannot be expected to make much headway in analyzing their own dreams, including a single dream.

Even people who are highly motivated and psychologically-minded may run into problems on dream analysis. They may have difficulty in free-associating on dream details or on the dream as a whole. They may, also, want to conclude that the dream stimulus was some trivial current event rather than an event which meant more to them than they realized because it mobilized some deeper psychological issues that had been silent. Or it reminded them of some distantly related psychological matters with which they were struggling.

With firm determination to know oneself, many of these obstacles can be overcome and steady progress can be made towards getting enlightening glimpses of oneself through dream analysis. Through regular contact with this facet of one's mental processes, dream analysis can contribute to a better appreciation of one's identity and potentiality and can lend a feeling of relative stability and familiarity to the otherwise large variety of unpredictable and confusing thoughts and feelings that may bombard our mental life.

SELECTED READINGS

Alexander, Franz. *The Scope of Psychoanalysis.* New York: Basic Books, 1961.

Altman, Leon L. *The Dream in Psychoanalysis.* New York: International Universities Press, 1969.

Dement, William C. *Some Must Watch While Some Must Sleep.* Stanford, Calif.: Stanford Alumni Association, 1972.

French, Thomas M. and Fromm, Erika. *Dream Interpretations: A New Approach.* New York: Basic Books, 1964.

Freud, Sigmund. *The Interpretation of Dreams.* New York: Basic Books, 1955 or Standard Edition, London: The Hogarth Press, 1959.

Jones, Richard M. *The New Psychology of Dreaming.* New York: Grune and Stratton, 1970.

INDEX

95

themes of, 32
as wish, 1
drugs, dreams and, 26

ego, 1-2, 4
ego ideal, 1, 4, 90
ego psychology, 6
emotional detachment, 7
erection, during sleep, 14

Fliess, W., 89
free-association, 35-36
dream analysis role, 5
Freud, S., vii, viii, 4, 5, 11, 19, 35, 69
self-analysis of dreams, 17-18, 89
fundamental rule, 35-36

humor, 8-9

id, 1, 2, 7

Jung, C., 20

Kleitman, 12

latent content, 4
LSD, 26

manifest content, 4

nightmare, repetitive, 79-80
"normal" thinking, 10

over-determination theory, 19-21

phobic defense, 8
primary process thinking, 2,4
projection, 7
psychiatric therapy, goals, 10-11

rapid eye-movement (REM), 12-15
reaction-formulation, 7
regression, 6,7
repression, 7
as obstacle in dream self-analysis, 89-91

safety in numbers mechanism, 9
secondary elaboration, 5
secondary process thinking, 2-3
self, turning against, 8
Seven Deadly Sins, 90
sleep, stages of, 12
sleepwalking, 14
sublimation, 6-7
suicide, dream related to, 46-48
superego, 1, 2, 90
supernatural, dreams as manifestations of, vii, 9-10
symbolization, 26-28
defined, 3
in psychological conflict of dreams, 4

Ten Commandments, 90
themes, dream, 23, 25, 32
tranquilizers, 26

unconscious, dreams as key to, vii-viii
undoing, 7-8

wish, dream as representative of, 1
wit, as psychological mechanism, 8-9